WHAT M.

by
PHILIP SEYER
Seyer Associates

ALLAN B. NOVICK
Musicologist

PAUL HARMON
Harmon Associates

Forest Hill Music

25 Balceta Ave.
San Francisco, CA 94127
Internet: http://www.ilovemusic.com
email: music@ilovemusic.com
phone: 415-665-8933

Cataloging in Publication Data

Seyer, Philip C., 1941-
    What Makes music work.

        Includes index.
        1. Music—Theory, Elementary. I. Novick,
Allan. II. Harmon, Paul. III. Title. IV. Series
MT7.S387   781   81-4930

Printed in the United States of America

10 9 8 7 6 5 4 3 2

How to Use This Book

Since this book is designed for self-study, questions and problems are interspersed throughout to give you a chance to apply what you are learning. The correct answer follows each item so you can check your work as you progress through the book.

We suggest that you cover the correct answer with a sheet of paper while you are reading the text and writing your answer. You may wish to use a "Post-It" index card for this purpose. These cards, available in stationery stores, have an adhesive backing so that they will stay in place when you put them over the answer. Yet you can easily remove them when you are ready to check your work.

Most of the time you will be right. If you find that you have made a mistake, you may wish to correct your answer with a red pen (pretending that you are your own teacher). This will be helpful if you want to review your work later.

When you correct your work, make sure you understand why the answer given is correct. If necessary, reread the preceding instructional material.

Space is provided in this book for you to write out your answers. But you may wish to buy some music writing paper (available in music stores) especially if you start arranging or composing your own music.

There are a lot of special musical terms to learn. If you forget the meaning of a musical term, you can refresh your memory by rereading the pages given for that term in the index at the back of the book.

Internet Music Teacher
If you have email and are connected to the Internet, you get a free music teacher when you buy this book. Just send questions or comments to music@ilovemusic.com – or visit:

http://www.ilovemusic.com

Preface

We designed this book for adults who have just recently decided to learn how music works. We start from scratch explaining basic things like note values, pitches, and time signatures. Then we progress to more difficult concepts like musical structure and harmonic movement.

We focus on contemporary popular music as well as on traditional Western music. By "contemporary popular" music, we mean music that is recorded and frequently played on the radio or purchased in music stores: rock n' roll, easy rock, Country and Western, New Age Music, slow romantic songs, and so on.

ACKNOWLEDGMENTS

We would like to thank these people for helping to bring *What Makes Music Work* to life:

- Akira and Yukiko Goto and Kumiko Seyer (for support and encouragement)

- Lea Smoot (for editorial help)

- Neuman Powell, Valparaiso University, Valparaiso Indiana (for his highly effective ideas on how to teach musical notation)

- Emeline Seyer, Herman Seyer, Miriam Tietjen, and Letha Wayne for support and enouragment.

- Jim Eilers and Nickie Gunstrom (for help in manuscript preparation)

Prelude

Have you ever wondered what makes certain music sound
- —wild and unrestrained
- —gentle and lilting
- —smooth and sweet
- . . .while other music sounds energetic, biting, or "spacy"?

Have you ever wondered how
- —a melody hangs together?
- —certain notes go together in harmony?
- —chord changes work?

Would you like to know what those funny numbers mean at the beginning of a piece of music? What a chord is? How chords are made? What *syncopation*, *dissonance*, or *motive* are? How to read music? What goes on in musicians' heads when they see B-flat?

If you've answered yes to any of these, this book is for you! It will take you step by step on a journey through the rudiments of music so that by the end of it you may surprise yourself by writing an original composition, complete with chord progressions, those funny numbers, and other musical symbols. We hope you'll enjoy the trip. Let's begin now with a study of musical notation.

Contents

How to Use This Book   3

Preface   4

Acknowledgments   4

Prelude   5

1 Reading and Writing Musical Pitch   7

2 Rhythm   27

3 Tempo and Meter   44

4 Scales   69

5 Intervals   104

6 Tonality   136

7 Musical Form and Design   160

8 Chords   190

9 Chord Progression and Harmonization   219

Appendix   251

Index   253

CHAPTER ONE

Reading and Writing Musical Pitch

You can learn to use a set of symbols to convey musical ideas—the same symbols composers use. These symbols are called musical notation. Since music is an organization of sounds and silences in time, notation does two things: It shows (1) the *pitch* of the sounds and (2) the *duration* of the sounds and silences in proper order. Pitch refers to the "highness" or "lowness" of a tone. A fog horn, for example, has a relatively low pitch, and a police whistle has a relatively high one. In this chapter you will learn to use musical notation to show pitch.

When you finish this chapter, you'll be able to

- Recognize and write the G-clef and F-clef signs
- Identify and write any note on a staff
- Use common accidentals to raise or lower a note
- Identify and write each of the common accidentals, including , ,♯,♭♭,𝄪, and ♮
- Identify the enharmonic spellings of any pitch

NOTES AND THE STAFF

Musicians write music on a set of five lines called a *staff*. The lines are always numbered from the bottom up, like this:

Staff

Notes (representing tones) are written on the staff. Some notes go on lines, like this:

Others go on spaces, like this:

The vertical placement of the notes on the staff shows the pitch of the tones represented by the notes. The first note in this example is higher (in pitch) than the second note.

Most notes have two parts, a note head and a stem.

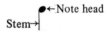

(You may have noticed that sometimes the stems go up and sometimes down. We'll explain why later.)

Which line or space is the first note on? The second note? Which note is *lower* in pitch?

_ _ _ _ _ _ _ _ _ _ _ _ _ _

The first note is on the fourth line; the second, on the fourth space. The first note is lower in pitch.

Clefs And Letter Names

Different musical pitches are given letter names to distinguish them from one another. This note is called G:

We know it is a G because the letter G is written on the second line and the note also appears on the second line. This G written at the beginning of the staff is called a *G-clef*. Today musicians use a fancy version of the letter G that looks like this:

You have probably seen this musical symbol somewhere before. Now you know what it means. The G-clef used to be placed on different lines at different times. This example shows the first line as G because the clef curls around the first line:

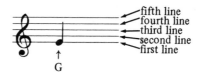

(Remember, these lines are always counted from the bottom up.)

Today the G-clef always curls around the *second* line of the staff, so whenever a G-clef is used, we know immediately that the second line is G.

Which note is G?

– – – – – – – – – – – – – –

The second note is G.

The F-Clef

The F-clef is made up of a curved line and two dots.

𝄢

To help yourself remember what an F-clef looks like, notice that if you were to connect the dots to the curved line you would get an ornate F. When the F-clef is used to show the location of the F note, one dot goes above the F line and one dot below it.

According to positioning of the F-clef, which line is the F line?

_ _ _ _ _ _ _ _ _ _ _ _ _ _ _ _

The fourth line, (from the bottom, of course). Today the F-clef always designates the fourth line as F.

Ledger Lines

When you want to write a pitch that is higher or lower than the staff, you add a line called a *ledger line*. Notice in this next illustration that the note sails over the top of the G-clef. To extend the range of the G-clef upwards, we simply add one or more short ledger lines above it.

An important note to piano players is *middle C*. It is called that because it is the C that appears in the middle of the keyboard. Middle C is written with a ledger line below the G-clef.

We can also write middle C with a ledger line *above* the F-clef.

The Grand Staff

As you know, a piano keyboard has lots of keys—eighty-eight to be exact! You may have been wondering how we could show that many notes on only a five-line staff even with ledger lines. What we do is use a grand staff. The *grand staff* is formed by connecting the G and F clefs by a brace. Notice how the alphabet goes up from middle C to G and then starts over with A. Also, notice how when you go down the staff, the letters progress in reverse alphabetical order.

Here you see how the notes on the grand staff relate to the piano keyboard. Directly below each key is the note that corresponds to it along with the letter designation for that key.

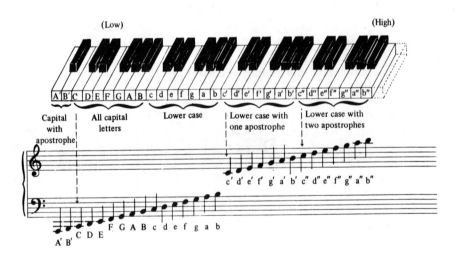

Letter Designations

Sometimes it is convenient to designate a specific musical tone (or its corresponding piano key) with a single letter rather than with a note on the staff. Study the previous diagram. Notice that we use capital letters for the lower tones. As the tones get higher, we use lower case letters. Beginning with middle C, we add a prime. Primes (using the apostrophe as its symbol) are added for each repetition of a letter (or tone). As the tones get higher still we add more primes. Here are some examples:

Throughout this book we use this system for distinguishing various pitches, so it is important for you to learn it.

Place a notation on this grand staff to show the pitch of each of these tones:

(1) A   (2) C′   (3) e″   (4) f

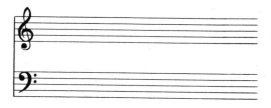

- - - - - - - - - - - - - - - -

Remembering the Lines and Spaces

To remember the names of the lines and spaces on the staff, some people find it helpful to think of words. For example the letters for the spaces of the staff with a G-clef spell "face."

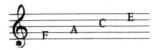

Looking at just the lines, we see

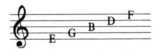

To remember these pitches we suggest you focus on the G line (which is always shown by the G-clef) and then develop a mental picture of the rest of the lines. Some people use the sentence "*Every Good Boy Does Fine*" to remember these lines. We do not recommend this because it takes too long to recall the letters this way. When reading music you must be able to recall the letter names instantly without having to recite a sentence first.

Take a good look at the letters for the G-clef staff. Then close your eyes and see if you can see them in your mind's eye. Then recall the letter name of each of these lines and spaces.

The F-clef staff

Now let's learn the letter names for the F-clef staff. It may help you to visualize the spaces of the F-clef as space "ace + G."

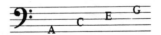

It may help you to see the lines in relation to the first three spaces (which spell "ace").

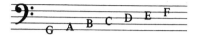

What are the letter names for these notes?

– – – – – – – – – – – – – – – – – –

(1) B   (2) g   (3) f   (4) A   (5) G   If you had trouble identifying the second note, notice that it is just above the F line; hence it is g (the next letter in the alphabet).

Now let's try some notes in the G-clef.

Label these notes with their letter names, written as capitals, lower case, or with primes.

The Musical Alphabet and the Octave

As we've seen from previous examples, the musical alphabet starts with A and goes up to G. The same is true on the piano keyboard. After G, the alphabet is repeated, it starts again with A.

As you've just learned, we can distinguish between notes by using capital letters, lower case letters, and primes. If we had a piano to play for you right now, and we played the white key on the far left of the keyboard, we would be playing A″. This is the lowest note on the piano; it has an almost growling sound. If we were to play a′ it would sound different—higher in pitch. Yet both notes would have a uniquely similar quality. If you were to play both a′ and a″ together at the same time, it might be difficult (if you didn't listen carefully) to tell that two different notes were sounding. Similarly all notes designated as B (whether B or b″, for example) have a similar quality; they all sound like B. When we want to refer to the letter name of a pitch in a general way, without specifying an exact location, we'll use a capital letter.

The Octave

The distance from one pitch to the next pitch with the same letter name is an *octave*. In other words, the distance from A″ to A′ is an octave, B″ to B′ is an octave and so on. The word octave comes from the root word *oct*, meaning eight (an *oct*opus has eight legs). That's because an octave includes eight white keys. Start with C as 1, and count to 8, or c.

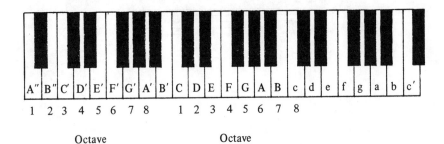

Men's and women's voices tend to be about an octave apart. In fact, if you play a note on the piano such as g' and ask a woman and man to sing it, the woman will almost invariably sing g', but the man will sing g (an octave lower than the actual pitch). That's because the lower octave is usually in a more comfortable part of a man's singing range.

(1) Put X on the key that is an octave above the key we have designated below.

↑ Put an 'x' on the key that is an octave above this key.

(2) How many white keys are in an octave?

_ _ _ _ _ _ _ _ _ _ _ _ _ _ _ _

(1)

Octave

(2) Eight

ACCIDENTALS: FLATS AND SHARPS

Notation evolved during the centuries when music generally made use of what are now the "white-key" pitches of the piano. So the pitches designated by lines and spaces on the staff correspond to white keys on the piano, as you can see here.

When our musical ancestors of the Middle Ages began playing a series of notes starting with f, they would make a change in one of the tones to get rid of what they considered a harsh sound.

You try it. (Borrow a friend's keyboard instrument if you need to.)

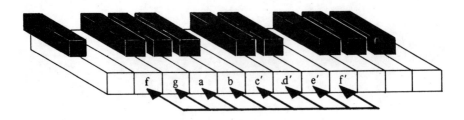

(1) Play these white keys on the piano or other instrument.

(2) Which key seems harsh?

Even today most people hear the tone B as "harsh" when this series of tones is played.

Flats

To avoid this harsh-sounding B, musicians lowered the pitch. They indicated that the B was to be lowered by placing the symbol ♭ *in front* of the note, like this:

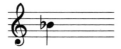

This symbol looks somewhat like a lower case b. Notice, however, that the shape is slightly different: the bottom is pointed.

Today this symbol is called a *flat sign*. It is used not only with b, but with all other letter designations to show that a tone is to be lowered in pitch.

When the flat sign is placed on a line, the staff line runs through the center of the sign's loop.

When the flat appears in a space, the loop fills the entire space.

When writing about pitches with letters, we put the flat sign after the letters.

C ♭ (C-flat)
D♭ (D-flat)

But when we use notes, we put the flat sign in front of the notes.

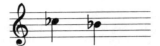

A flat sign in front of a tone lowers the tone one half step to the next lower tone. On the piano, this means the tone is moved to the next key to the left—whether the key is black or white.

On the diagram of this piano keyboard, indicate which keys you would use to play these notes:

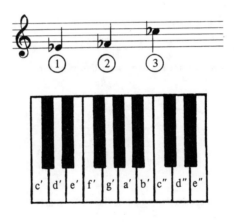

- - - - - - - - - - - - - -

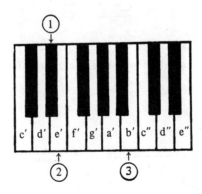

Did you have trouble with f'♭ and c"♭ in the last exercise? If so, remember that a flat sign lowers a tone to the next lower tone. In other words, start with the tone (without the flat), and then move to the next lower tone. This lower tone may correspond to either a white key or a black key.

As you have seen, F♭ is really the same as E. So C♭ is the same as what pitch?

— — — — — — — — — — — — — —

B

Sharp Signs

Just as a flat sign (♭) lowers a pitch, a sharp sign (♯) raises a pitch to the next higher pitch. On the piano, this means moving to the next key on the right (whether white or black).

When you write a sharp sign on a staff line, the line should go through the sharp's center.

 (F♯)

If you write it on a space, the sharp's middle box would fill up the space.

 (C♯)

What keys would you use to play these notes?

Show your answer on this diagram:

— — — — — — — — — — — — — —

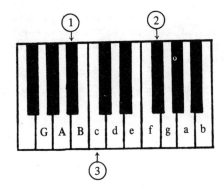

ENHARMONIC EQUIVALENTS

Two notes (like Fb and E) that have different names but designate the same pitch are called *enharmonic equivalents*. Here's another example:

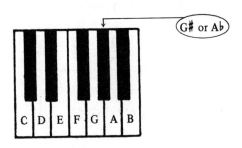

As you can see, both G♯ and Ab correspond to the same piano key. Which of the following pairs of notes are enharmonic equivalents? (Use a keyboard diagram if you need to.)

(1) Cb and B
(2) Db and C♯
(3) Ab and F♯

– – – – – – – – – – – – – – –

(1) and (2)

Natural Signs

When a flat or sharp sign no longer applies to a line or space on the staff—when the pitch is returned to its original or "natural" state— a *natural sign* (♮) appears in front of the note. Thus to raise a note that was previously lowered with a flat sign, you put a natural sign before it.

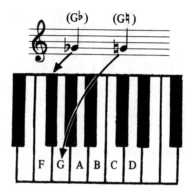

You also use a natural sign to *lower* a note that has been previously raised.

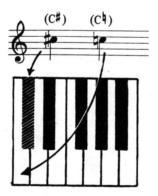

Double-Sharps and Double-Flats

Musical signs like sharps and flats that are used to raise and lower pitches are called *accidentals*. There are two more accidental signs you need to learn to use. They do the same thing as sharps and flats; they raise and lower a pitch to its next higher or lower neighbor. But these signs represent a pitch that has been raised or lowered twice; so these signs are called *double-sharp* and *double-flat*.

D♯ is a D raised to its next higher tone. You can raise it still further by making it a D-double-sharp. The symbol for a double-sharp is an x written in front of the note.

(Notice that D^x is really the same as E.)

A double sharp may also be written with two sharps in front of a note. So instead of writing

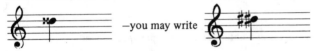

—you may write

To lower a flattened pitch still further to its next lower neighbor pitch, the sign changes from flat (♭) to double-flat (♭♭). For example, an E♭ is an E lowered to its next lower tone. You can lower it further by making it E-double-flat. (Notice that E♭♭ is the same pitch as D.)

(1) Write a G-clef on this staff. Then indicate these pitches with noteheads (don't use stems): f″♭♭, c‴##, g′, d″♭

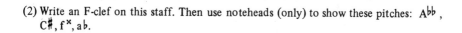

(2) Write an F-clef on this staff. Then use noteheads (only) to show these pitches: A♭♭, C#, f×, a♭.

(3) Show which piano keys you would use to play these notes:

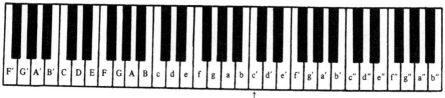

Middle C

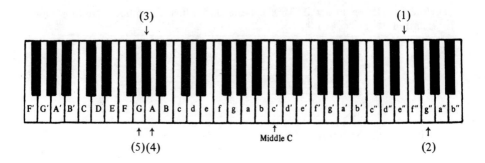

If you missed the notes in item (3), notice that there is an F-clef before the third note, so these notes must be read in the F-clef.

Now that you're familiar with the notation of pitch, it's time to look at notation of another important part of music—rhythm.

CHAPTER TWO

Rhythm

In the previous chapter, you saw how the vertical placement of musical symbols on the staff shows pitch. The horizontal placement of symbols, going from left to right, shows the succession of sounds and silences in musical time. For Examples (a) and (b) contain exactly the same notes, but they are musically different. That's because the horizontal placement of the notes is different, and because (b) contains a *silence* indicated by the symbol ≯ .

silence

This chapter is concerned with rhythm and its notation. Rhythm refers to the specific length of each sound and silence in music. We identify the duration of a tone, as well as its pitch, with a *note*. We indicate the duration of silences with *rests*.

When you finish this chapter, you'll be able to

- Give the name for each of these kinds of notes:

- Identify the rest that corresponds to each kind of note
- Use ties and dots to show the time values of notes
- Explain why American musicians find it easy to recognize stop signs in Italy that say "fermata"

● Carry out a rhythmical exercise in which you simultaneously tap out these note values: (in one-person-band style)

Duration

Besides showing pitch, notes can also show how long a tone lasts; that is, they can show the duration of a tone. The longest note-value commonly used is the whole note, shown by an oval. Successively shorter notes use stems and flags.

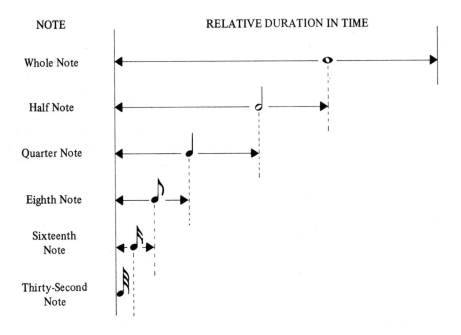

NOTE	RELATIVE DURATION IN TIME
Whole Note	
Half Note	
Quarter Note	
Eighth Note	
Sixteenth Note	
Thirty-Second Note	

The actual duration of a note is based on the beat. A beat is simply a regular pulsation that divides musical time into equal units. Examine the different kinds of notes. Notice that a half note lasts half as long as a whole note. The quarter note, in turn, lasts half as long as a half note. Does this pattern continue?   Yes ___   No ___

— — — — — — — — — — — — — — — —

Yes. Each successive shorter note is equal to half the value of the preceding note.

The duration of notes *in relation to each other* is fixed: the half note is half the value of the whole note, no matter what the actual length of time the whole note will sound. This is a system of *relative* time value.

This will become clear as we study each of the different notes in more detail. Let's begin with the whole note.

The *whole note* is written as an oval. It is generally the longest note value used in modern music.

One whole note is equal in value to two half notes. We can show this using notes as:

Notice that the *half note* is made by attaching a *stem* to the oval.

Application

We can use two half notes and a whole note to show the rhythm of the spoken words *slowing down*. We'll let each word, *slowing* and *down*, take up the same amount of time. Since *slowing* has two syllables, each syllable will occupy exactly one-half the time of *down*. Look at this illustration and notice how two half notes and a whole note can be used to show this time relation.

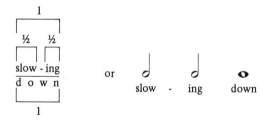

First, let's establish a pace. You can do that by tapping your foot slowly and evenly. When you've established a slow steady pace (the beat), say "down" each time your foot strikes the floor. Make sure that you stretch out the pronunciation of the word so that it fills up all the time between one foot-tap and the next.

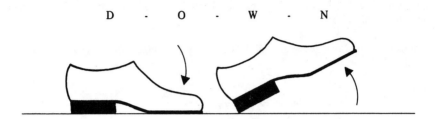

We can write these foot-taps musically using whole notes.

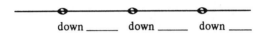

When you feel comfortable saying "down" to the same steady tap of your foot, continue without changing pace, and with your finger add two *even* taps for each tap of your foot. The finger-taps should evenly divide the time between one foot-tap and the other.

Look at this illustration and the notes below to see whether you did the application correctly.

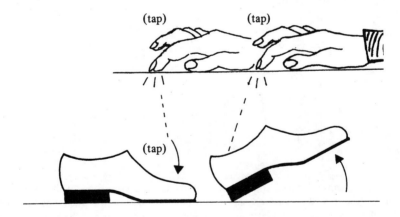

Notice that your first finger-tap occurs exactly when your foot strikes the floor. Your second finger-tap occurs when your foot starts to move upward.

Since each of the faster taps is exactly half the value of the foot-taps, we can represent the faster taps by half notes.

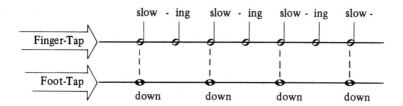

In reading this notation, let your eyes move once across the page from left to right. Read the finger-tap notation simultaneously with the foot-tap notation.

Here, the half notes match the two syllables of the word *slowing*. When you feel comfortable maintaining two of the steady, even finger-taps for each of the foot-taps, add "slow-ing down—slow-ing down—." Match *slowing* to a pair of half notes (the finger-taps, and *down* to a whole note (the foot-tap). Change your mental focus from your finger-taps to your foot-taps, like this:

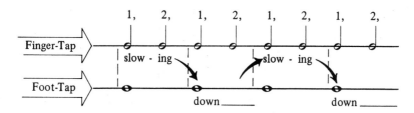

When you say "down—" you may have a tendency to stop tapping your fingers. Don't stop. You might need to slow down the pace. Keep the finger tapping as you focus on the slower foot-tap.

Quarter Notes

A half note can be divided into two *quarter notes*. This is written as

Quarter notes are shown as black notes with stems.

In printed music, quarter notes look almost like half notes that have been colored in.

half note   quarter note

When *writing* music by hand, with a pencil, however, experienced musicians often make quarter notes like this:

Notice that the colored-in oval is replaced by a dark slanted line. You may wish to use this style in doing the exercises in this book. It will save you time and make your work look more professional.

With the quarter notes added to our repertory of note values, we can notate a more varied rhythmical phrase.

Application

Let's try another tapping exercise. First, with your pencil or finger, tap a steady beat at a pace you might comfortably walk to—not slow and not fast. We can write these taps using quarter notes organized in groups of four. So you feel the grouping of taps in four, *stress* the first of every four taps by striking the table harder.

It is important to stress the first of every four taps because this will help you coordinate this finger tapping with the foot tapping, which comes later. When you've set up a steady pace, say "walk-ing eas-y" to each group of four taps, one syllable to a tap.

Next we will add to the quarter notes two half notes. Tap your foot at the beginning of each word. Tap your foot twice to every group of four quarter notes beats. Repeat the phrase three times. Follow this illustration.

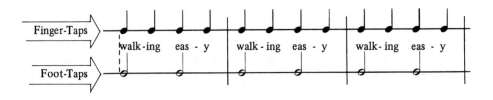

Notice that this time each foot-tap is represented by a half note. Let's now add *walking easy* to the earlier phrase *slowing down*. This means that to the group of four quarter notes, we will add two half note taps, then one whole note. The whole note is held for the value of the two half notes (or four quarters). Notice that in this exercise your speech slows down, but your fingers tap steadily in quarter notes and your foot taps steadily in half notes. To the notation below, we've added numbers to indicate your finger-taps and arrows to indicate your foot-taps.

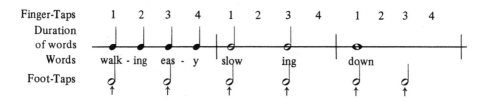

If you have the optional cassette tape accompanying this book, you may wish to do the rhythmic exercises at this time, which will give you added practice similar to that given here. (See Appendix on how to order it.)

Eighth Notes

A quarter note can be divided into two *eighth notes*. This can be written

You write an eighth note by attaching a flag to the stem of a quarter note. The flag always goes from the stem to the right, as illustrated below.

When eighth notes are written in groups a crossbar called a *beam* replaces a flag. This makes for easier reading.

beam
beam (notes moving down therefore beam slants down)

Notice that the direction of the beam coincides with the general direction of the pitch changes of the notes.

On the staff below, write the following notes:

(1) a single eighth note on G
(2) a single eighth note on g
(3) a group of four eighth notes on d, e, f, and a
(4) a sequence of four eighth notes on B, A, B, and B

- - - - - - - - - - - - - - - -

(1)   (2)   (3)   (4)

Quarter Note – Eighth Note Application

Tap your left foot at a slow easy pace (about one tap every second). We will notate these taps with quarter notes.

Left foot

tap   tap   tap   tap

Once your left foot is tapping along at an easy pace, begin tapping your right foot exactly twice as fast so that for every left foot-tap there are two right foot-taps.

Quarter note – Eighth Note – Sixteenth Note Application

In this exercise, you begin by tapping *slowly* with your left foot. Next add two taps with your right for each single tap with your left, as with the previous exercise:

When you have that rhythm going comfortably, begin tapping your left hand against your knee at a speed that is twice as fast as your *right* foot. We can write this tapping like this:

If you have difficulty keeping all three limbs going at the same time, try practicing any two separately. Also, go more slowly. For example, practice tapping four taps with your left hand for one tap with your left foot, or four taps with your left hand against two taps with your right foot. (If you have the optional cassette tape for this book, you will find it helpful in learning this exercise.) Now put your one-man rhythm band together:

—First establish a beat with your left foot, about once every two seconds. These are the quarter notes.

—Then add your right foot by tapping twice the speed of the left: two eighth-note taps to every quarter-note beat.

—Next, begin tapping sixteenth notes with your left hand, two taps to each tap of your right foot.

—Finally add your right hand rhythm by tapping the fastest speed (representing thirty-second notes), two taps to each tap of the left hand.

If you begin to lose track, stop and begin with a slower left-foot beat. Give yourself plenty of time by adding the different components gradually.

This will take some practice, but it is well worth the effort because it will give you a clear sense of the various note values involved. (It may take some time to master this one, so don't be discouraged.) When all four limbs are tapping at this slow pace, gradually speed up until your right hand is tapping away at a fairly rapid rate, say, four taps every second. (If you feel slightly ridiculous, you may want to be sure you're doing this exercise in private!)

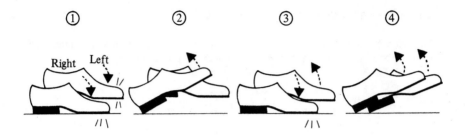

Both toes *strike* floor together.

Left toe stays on floor. Right toe lifts for second tap.

As right foot strikes floor for second tap, left foot starts to lift up.

Right foot lifts up, too (at a faster speed), so that both feet are *ready* to move back down and strike floor together repeating step 1.

We can write this musically as

Shorter Notes

Further subdivisions result in notes that have progressively shorter durations. An eighth note, for example, can be divided into two *sixteenth notes* and written

If the quarter note is moving at an easy walking speed, the sixteenth note brings us into the realm of fairly rapid sound. A sixteenth note is formed by adding a second flag to the stem of an eighth note or, if a series of notes are connected, adding a second beam.

You can also group sixteenth notes together to make them easier to read, as illustrated here:

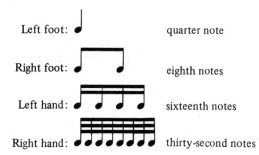

Left foot: quarter note

Right foot: eighth notes

Left hand: sixteenth notes

Right hand: thirty-second notes

The Rhythm Tree

Now that you have a feel for some of the basic note values, let's look at what is called a *rhythm tree*. It shows how two half notes equal a whole note and two quarter notes equal a half note, and so on. We have carried the tree through thirty-second notes.

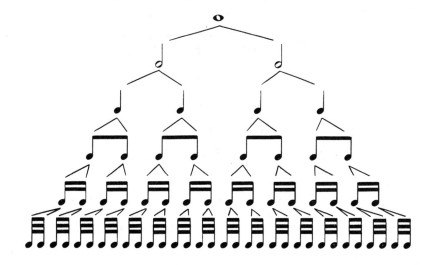

Study the rhythm tree to figure out how sixty-fourth notes would be written. On the staff below write eight sixty-fourth notes on f. (The stems should go down.)

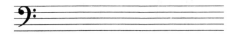

Let's Review

Give the time value name and letter name for each of these notes. (We've done the first one for you.)

(1) whole note on g″   (5) _____
(2) _____   (6) _____
(3) _____   (7) _____
(4) _____   (8) _____

- - - - - - - - - - - - - -

(1) whole note on g″   (5) quarter note on c′
(2) eighth notes on f″ and e″   (6) thirty-second notes on G
(3) half note on c″   (7) half note on B
(4) sixteenth note on a″   (8) eighth note on g

We can also use musical notation to *add* value to a note. So far we've only talked about note values that can be divided into smaller even-numbered units. If we wanted to notate a sound that lasted three-fourths the value of a whole note, we would have to combine the note values of one half note and one quarter note. We can do this by connecting them with a curved line called a *tie*. It is usually written on the opposite side from the note stems and does not quite touch the note heads. The most frequent combinations are those in which a note is tied to another note one half its value, as this creates a note three units long. (Remember that notes values smaller than a whole note are multiples of two.)

Assume that ♩ = one beat. How many beats should each of these tones be held for?

– – – – – – – – – – – – – – – – –

(1) five beats   (2) six beats   (3) eight beats

Assume that ♩ = one beat. Write out the notation needed to show that b' should be held for three beats.

– – – – – – – – – – – – – – – – –

   or

Dotted Notes

The *dot*, placed after the note head, is a more concise symbol than the tie. It shows a note value that you can divide into three equal units. *A dot increases the duration of a note by one-half its value.* In item (1) following, we show a dotted whole note and its corresponding value as tied notes. We also show the value of the dot. Do the same for each of the other notes in the list.

Dotted note	Tied notes	Note value the dot equals
(1) 𝅝 ·	= 𝅝 ⌣ 𝅗𝅥	dot = 𝅗𝅥
(2) 𝅗𝅥 ·	=	dot =
(3) 𝅘𝅥 ·	=	dot =
(4) 𝅘𝅥𝅮 ·	=	dot =
(5) 𝅘𝅥𝅯 ·	=	dot =

— — — — — — — — — — — — — — —

(2) 𝅗𝅥 ·	= 𝅗𝅥 ⌣ 𝅘𝅥 ;	dot = 𝅘𝅥
(3) 𝅘𝅥 ·	= 𝅘𝅥 ⌣ 𝅘𝅥𝅮 ;	dot = 𝅘𝅥𝅮
(4) 𝅘𝅥𝅮 ·	= 𝅘𝅥𝅮 ⌣ 𝅘𝅥𝅯 ;	dot = 𝅘𝅥𝅯
(5) 𝅘𝅥𝅯 ·	= 𝅘𝅥𝅯 ⌣ 𝅘𝅥𝅰 ;	dot = 𝅘𝅥𝅰

Rests

In music, pauses or silences between tones are equally as important as tones themselves. They are indicated by symbols called *rests*, which correspond to the time values of the notes we have just discussed. There are slight variations between the printed and written rests; both versions appear in the following table with the corresponding note value.

Note		Rest			Note	Rest	
		Printed	Written			Printed	Written
‖o‖	Double whole	■	(same)		♪ Eighth	𝄾	𝄾
o	Whole	▬	(same)		♬ 16th		
♩	Half	▬	(same)		32nd		
♩	Quarter	𝄽	𝄼		64th		

Notice that the whole rest hangs from a line while the half rest sits on a line. You might try remembering the difference by visualizing the half rest as a *half* of a top hat.

(top hat) ▮ (½ of a top hat)

Notice also that from the eighth rest on, each rest has the same number of crossmarks or dots as there are flags on the staff of the corresponding note.

Rests can be combined in any way: 𝄽 𝄾 or ▬ 𝄽 and no *tie* is necessary. They can also be dotted, like notes, to add the value of half its symbol.

▬• = ▬ 𝄽

𝄽• = 𝄽 𝄾

𝄾• = 𝄾 𝄾

In the opening of Beethoven's Fifth Symphony, notice that before each group of three eighth notes there is an eighth-note rest.

Beethoven's Fifth Symphony

The phrase actually begins with the silence which is the same duration as the eighth notes:

(Pause)-short-short-short-*long*
(Pause)-short-short-short-*long*

Fermata

American musicians traveling in Italy are often amused to find out that street stop signs say "fermata." A musical sign that indicates a certain kind of stop is also called *fermata* (*stop* in Italian). The note over which the fermata sign appears is held for longer than its actual note value. Here is a fermata sign, also called a "bird's eye" because it looks like one:

The length of the hold is not set, but depends on the taste of the performer and the style of the music. Fermatas often appear at the end of phrases or sections. You may be familiar with one of the more famous uses of the fermata in instrumental music, in the opening of the first movement of Beethoven's Fifth Symphony. The long note in the "short-short-short-*long*; short-short-short-*long*" pattern has a fermata and is held for different lengths in different performances.

Notes and Rests Application

Indicate whether the rests on the left are greater than >, smaller than <, or equal to = the notes or rests on the right. We have done the first one for you.

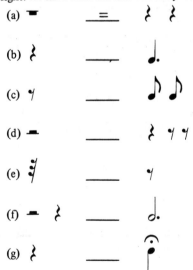

— — — — — — — — — — — — — —

(a) >
(b) <
(c) <
(d) =
(e) <
(f) =
(g) <

(The fermata adds an extra duration to the quarter note so that it is greater than a quarter rest.)

Now that you've got rhythm, you're ready to learn about meter and other aspects of musical time.

CHAPTER THREE

Tempo and Meter

In the last chapter we discussed the different kinds of notes, signs, and symbols used to show the relative duration of sounds and silences. You learned, for example, that a half note is twice as long as a quarter note. But you didn't learn how to determine the absolute duration of sounds and silences. You didn't learn, for example, how to determine how many quarter notes should occur in, say, one minute. You'll learn how in this chapter. In addition, you will learn the difference between beats and pulses and how musicians group beats into patterns with a system called meter.

When you finish this chapter you'll be able to

- Define pulse, meter, and tempo
- Recognize duple, triple, and quadruple meter, both simple and complex
- Identify and notate time signatures in both simple and compound meter
- Recognize asymmetric time
- Recognize syncopation
- Identify the kind of musicians who have a strong need for a conductor, and explain why they do

Beat and Tempo

A *beat* is a regular pulsation. A clock ticks to a regular beat all by itself. Conductors indicate beat to an orchestra by the up and down movements of their hands. In musical notation, beats are often organized into strong and weak beat patterns according to a system called *meter*. Meter measures musical time according to beat patterns. *Tempo* refers to the speed of the beat. In most popular music (such as rock, disco, new wave, jazz, swing, country and western) the tempo usually remains the same throughout a composition; the beat is steady, regular, almost unchanging—like the ticking of a clock. This characteristic makes it especially suitable for dancing: once the beat is established, the dancers can rely on it and concentrate on their footwork. In contrast, musicians performing "classical" music (by composers such as Bach, Beethoven, Brahms, Stravinsky) often take greater liberties with the beat and often subtly speed it up or slow it down.

Given that a conductor makes it easier for a group of musicians to observe the beat, which group do you think has more need for a conductor?

(1) A symphony orchestra
(2) A rock group

— — — — — — — — — — — — — — —

(1) A symphony orchestra

A symphony orchestra nearly always performs with a conductor. Since the beat changes often, the musicians need a conductor to give them a visual image of the beat so they can stay with it. It's crucial that these musicians keep one eye on their music and one eye on the conductor. If they don't, the conductor lets them know it quickly!

Musicians playing popular music, on the other hand, don't usually need a conductor, since once a beat is established it doesn't change (except at the very end of a piece when it may slow down.) That's why blind musicians can play with popular groups but not usually with symphonic orchestras.

Beats and Note Values

To determine how long to play each note we need to know what kind of note equals one beat. It can be any kind of note. We can say: "Let each eighth note equal one beat" or "Let a quarter note equal one beat." Whatever note is chosen determines the value of all other notes. If we let a quarter note equal one beat, then the other notes equal these values:

$$\text{♩} = 2 \text{ beats} \qquad \text{♪} = \text{½ beat}$$

$$\text{𝅝} = 4 \text{ beats} \qquad \text{♬} = \text{¼ beat}$$

But if an eighth note equals one beat, then

$$\text{♪} = \text{½ beat} \qquad \text{♩} = 4 \text{ beats}$$

$$\text{♩} = 2 \text{ beats} \qquad \text{𝅝} = 8 \text{ beats}$$

Suppose we let a half note equal one beat. How many beats (or parts of a beat) would each of these notes be equal to?

(1) 𝅝 = _____

(2) ♩ = _____

(3) ♪ = _____

- - - - - - - - - - - - - - -

(1) two
(2) one-half
(3) one-fourth

Meter: Patterns of Beat

Meter, we said earlier, is the organization of beats into patterns of strong and weak beats. We have a natural tendency to think metrically, that is, to group beats mentally into strong and weak beats.

If you have an old-fashioned watch that ticks, hold it to your ear. Do you hear a pattern? Is it TICK-tock? or TICK-tock-tock?

- - - - - - - - - - - - - - -

We rarely hear it as "tick-tick-tick-tick. . ." even though most clocks tick quite evenly. Most of us hear the ticks in groups of two, with the accent on the first beat: "TICK-tock, TICK-tock. . ." or "ONE-two, ONE-two. . ." We organize our walking beats the same way: LEFT-right, LEFT-right. Listen to the percussive clackety-clackety of a train and you'll hear those sounds in beat patterns too. Different people will hear different patterns, but the patterns will be there. CLACK-e-ty, CLACK-e-ty is only one possibility; it organizes the sounds into groups of three: ONE-two-three, ONE-two-three. Hearing sound as beat patterns is just one way in which we experience recurring cycles in our lives and in our world: the two-beat pattern of breathing, heartbeats, tides, day and night; the three-beat pattern of morning–noon–night; the four-beat pattern of winter–spring–summer–fall. We respond to patterns of sound and create them, both with little or no conscious effort.

Beat patterns come naturally to children; they respond wholeheartedly to the patterns in nursery rhymes by skipping, clapping, and dancing. Notice the beat patterns in these nursery rhymes. (We've added vertical lines to help you see the beat patterns.)

2-Beat Patterns	1 2	1 2	1 2	1 2
	JACK-and	JILL-went	UP- the	HILL- to...
	JACK-be	NIM- ble	JACK-be	QUICK...
	MAR- y	HAD-a	LIT- tle	LAMB-its

3-Beat Patterns	1 2 3	1 2 3	1 2 3	1 2 3
	ALL- the-king's	HORS-es and	ALL the king's	MEN – –
	COULD-n't put	HUMP-ty to-	GETH-er a-	GAIN – –

Measures and Bar Lines

In music, groups of notes or units of musical time are separated. The *bar lines* divide the music into tiny segments called *measures* (or bars).

bar lines

Measure
(bar)

These measures make it easier for musicians to keep track of where they are while reading music. The bars also show the beat patterns. A bar-line signals the end of a beat pattern and the start of a new (usually identical) pattern.

Time Signature

A *time signature* shows the meter of a piece of music. It consists of two numbers, one written above the other; on the staff it appears just after the clef sign and just before the first measure. The top number shows the *number* of notes per measure. The bottom number tells *what kind* of notes (whether half notes, whole notes, quarter notes, etc.). In the following figure, of a time signature of $\frac{3}{4}$ means that there are three quarter notes in every measure (or the equivalent in notes and rests).

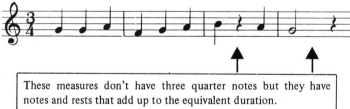

These measures don't have three quarter notes but they have notes and rests that add up to the equivalent duration.

Notice that the 4 in the time signature of $\frac{3}{4}$ stands for quarter notes. A time signature of $\frac{3}{8}$ would mean that every measure contains three eighth notes (or the equivalent in notes and rests.)

What kind of time signature would show that each measure contains the equivalent of three half notes?

– – – – – – – – – – – – – –

Part of the time signature is given for each of these examples. Supply the missing number in each case.

(1) $\frac{2}{7}$

(2) $\frac{4}{2}$

(3) $\frac{6}{8}$

If you had difficulty with (3), remember that ♩. = ♪♪♪ . Therefore, ♩. + ♩. = six eighth notes or $\frac{6}{8}$.

Different Kinds of Meter

It is useful to be able to recognize the different kinds of time signatures because you will be better able to read music written in various meters. It's also fun when listening to music to pick out the different metrical patterns that are occurring. A knowledge of time signatures will help you do this.

Simple Meter

A meter is *simple* when its beat is divided in *half.*

- When the top number in the key signature is 2, the meter is called *simple duple* (duple means two), as in $\frac{2}{8}$.
- When the top number in the key signature is 3, the meter is called *simple triple*, as in $\frac{3}{16}$.
- When the top number in the key signature is 4, the meter is called *simple quadruple*, as in $\frac{4}{4}$.

Compound Meter

A meter is *compound* when its beat is divided in *thirds.*

- When the top number, divided by 3, comes out to
  Two—the meter is *compound duple*, as in $\frac{6}{4}$.
  Three—the meter is *compound triple*, as in $\frac{9}{8}$.
  Four—the meter is *compound quadruple*, as in $\frac{12}{4}$.

Here are some examples. Part of the time signature is given for each one. Put in the missing numbers for each and tell what kind of meter it is.

- - - - - - - - - - - - - - - -

Answers:

(1) $\frac{9}{8}$ Compound triple

(2) $\frac{6}{8}$ Compound duple

(3) $\frac{3}{16}$ Simple triple

(4) $\frac{4}{4}$ Simple quadruple

Beats per Measure

The number of beats per measure is partly up to the discretion of the performing musician or conductor. It's important to decide how many beats will occur in one measure, because your musical performance will be affected by this decision. If you put too many beats in a measure, the music may sound too plodding, or mechanical. If you put in too few beats the music may lack precision or it may not give the energetic impression intended by the composer. In making this decision it's important to refer to the time signature.

Often—but *not always*—the top number of the time signature tells how many beats should occur per measure. If the time signature says $\frac{3}{4}$ the performer may put three beats in every measure and let the quarter note equal one beat. Sometimes, however, a performer will take the tempo so fast that an entire measure will equal one beat. Then each quarter note is considered to be a pulse or subdivision of the beat.[1]

Whenever the meter is *duple*, the performer should consider putting two beats per measure, since the term *duple* suggests two beats or at least two groupings of beats. For example, if you have a compound duple meter of **§**, consider putting two beats in every measure, as in this example:

I   want   to   share   my   life   with   you!

ONE   TWO   ONE   TWO

Beats

In the example above in **§** time what is the value of one beat? (Pick one.)

(1) ♩

(2) ♪

(3) ♩.

_ _ _ _ _ _ _ _ _ _ _ _ _ _

(3) Notice that each beat consists of three eighth notes (or the equivalent, which is a dotted quarter note).

Even though there are only two beats per measure in the example above, there are six pulses per measure. A *pulse*, as we define it, is similar to a beat except that it is lighter and faster. (You can tap your foot to the beat, but you only feel the pulse.) In this case each eighth note equals one pulse. Sometimes musicians may count the pulses in **§** time like this (saying the numbers *one* and *four* much louder than the others):

_ _ _ _ _ _ _ _ _ _ _ _ _ _

[1]See: Willi Apel, *The Harvard Dictionary of Music* (Cambridge, Mass.: Harvard University Press, 1965), p. 81. Some music teachers make the mistake of teaching that the top number always tells the number of beats per measure. It doesn't!

(Pulses) 1 2 3 4 5 6

Pulses one and four are much stronger than the rest because they occur right on the beat:

Pulses: 1 2 3 4 5 6

Beat: 1 - - 2 - -

(Perhaps you can see more clearly now why **8̸** is called compound duple: because each beat may be broken down into *three* pulses, each of which can be represented by an eighth note.)

A time signature of **8̸** doesn't always have two beats per measure. If the tempo (speed of the beat) is slow, each eighth note may equal one beat. Then there would be six beats per measure. The top number in time signature can indicate either the number of *beats* or the number of *pulses* per measure.

"Silent Night" is written in **8̸** time. Examine the excerpt below as you hum the melody to yourself. Try to feel the beat. Do you think there should be two or six beats per measure?

How many beats per measure?

— — — — — — — — — — — — — — —

Six. (each eighth note equals one beat.)

Thus, when the meter is duple, consider putting two beats to the measure. But be aware that more (or fewer) beats may be appropriate.

In the same way consider putting three beats to the measure with a piece in triple meter. For example:

But also consider giving it just *one* beat per measure as would occur in a rapid tempo.

If there is one beat per measure in 𝟑/𝟒 time, what is the value of one beat? One pulse?

– – – – – – – – – – – – –

Each beat equals ♩. (or ♩ ♩ ♩). Each pulse equals ♩ .

Quadruple meter often has four beats per measure. But this may be cut to two beats per measure. This is sometimes referred to as cut time[1]. Tempo (the speed of the beat) is usually the determining factor when it comes to deciding how many beats to put to a measure. (Of course, you still need to consider the time signature.) You can tap your foot (as a performer) or wave your arms (as a conductor) only so fast. If the tempo is fast, it is often easier and less tiring to beat fewer beats per measure. Also, with fewer beats per measure the performance comes out smoother, less choppy.

On the other hand, with a very slow tempo, musicians tend to put in more beats per measure. Instead of letting, say, a quarter note get the beat, they may give a beat to every eighth note. Since tempo is such an important factor in musical performance, let's discuss the way musicians notate it.

Tempo

In written music, tempo markings appear above the staff at the beginning and whenever the tempo (or speed) changes. The tempo indication can appear in two ways.

---

[1]Quadruple meter is also called *common time* because it occurs so often. Cut time has the four beats cut to two, and is indicated by the time signature ¢ (for common time). Each of the two beats has the value of a half note.

Speed and speed changes indicated by words.

The first method is to use words to indicate the general speed. In the seventeenth century, when tempo markings first came into style, Italian musicans dominated the European musical scene. They left a vocabulary for a wide range of *tempi* (the Italian plural of *tempo*). Here are some of the most important of these Italian terms.

Table 3-1

FAST	*Allegro*	fast
	Allegro con brio [BREE-o]	fast, with brilliance
	Allegro con spirito	fast, with spirit
	Presto	very fast
	Vivace [vee-VAH-chey]	lively
MEDIUM	*Andante* [on-DON-tey]	moderately; literally "going over," "walking"
	Moderato	moderately
SLOW	*Lento*	slowly
	Grave [GRA-vey]	heavily, seriously, very slowly
	Adagio [a-DA-jo]	slowly, drawn out; very slow
	Largo [LAR-go]	broadly, very slow

These Italian terms above can be modified by the following words, which define more precisely the tempo desired by the composer.

meno [MAY-no]	less
non troppo	not too much
poco	a little
molto	very

For example, *Molto largo* means "very, very slow."

Table 3-2

-ino *-etto*	These diminutive endings (meaning less, or small) can be added to one of the basic tempo markings to indicate *less* of the basic quality: *allegretto*—not too fast, less fast; or *larghetto* —not so broadly, slowly, less slowly.
-issimo	An augmentive ending, meaning "very much" or "a lot," when added to a tempo marking, indicates an *increase* or *more* of a particular quality: *prestissimo* [pres-TEE-see-mo] —as fast as possible.

Tempo Variation

As we discussed earlier, classical music often speeds up or slows down. Variation in tempo can occur at any moment in a piece of music. The terms below indicate tempo variation.

Table 3-3

FASTER	*accelerando* [ah-che-le-RAN-do]	getting faster, accelerating
	più [pew]	used to indicate "more": *più allegro—* "more" allegro, faster.
	più mosso	"more movement," faster
	stringendo [strin-JEN-do]	rushing
SLOWER	*meno* [MAY-no]	used with a tempo indication, means "less": *meno adagio*—not so slowly as before.
	meno mosso	slower, "less movement"
	rallentando (abbr.: *rall.*)	slowing down
	ritardando	slow down, retard, hold back (momentary; whereas *rallentando* occurs over a longer period of time)
	ritenuto (*rit.*)	held back
a tempo		"at speed," back to the main speed (after slowing down or speeding up)
tempo primo *tempo I°*		first speed; back to the first tempo when some other has intervened
L'istesso tempo		the same speed; confirming the continuance of the same tempo

Speed indication by metronome markings

Some composers use a *metronome* to show the tempo precisely. A metronome is a time-piece invented in the early nineteenth century that makes a ticking sound for any speed at which it is set. Beethoven was one of the first to use it. Metronome speeds are indicated by numbers that measure notes per minute.

Sometimes tempo speeds are written at the beginning of a piece and include a note value and a number that stands for the number of notes per minute. For example, if a composer wants the music to move at the rate of sixty quarter notes per minute, you will see: ♩ = 60

Estimating Tempo

With a little practice you can learn to estimate quickly the tempo of a musical perfor-mance. First listen to the music and snap your fingers, or tap your foot, or slap your thigh (not too hard!) to the beat. Then, using a watch with a second hand, count the number of beats in ten seconds. Then multiply by 6 to find the number of beats per minute.

Application

Listen to various kinds of music on the radio.

(1) What is the fastest beat that you hear? _____
(2) The slowest? _____
(3) Using the estimating technique, give the typical tempo (in beats per minute) for each of these kinds of pieces:
    (a) A slow romantic popular song like "Yesterday" by the Beatles.
    (b) A disco number like "Stayin' Alive."
    (c) The fast section of an orchestral composition (like Beethoven's Fifth Symphony).
    (d) A fast rock 'n' roll song like "I Wanna Hold Your Hand" by the Beatles.

– – – – – – – – – – – – – – –

(1) The fastest tempo you are likely to hear will be between about 150 and 180 beats per minute. Beats faster than 180 per minute tend to be treated as subdivision pulses of the beat rather than beats. Remember, you can tap your foot only so fast! If what seems to be the beat is going so fast that you can't tap your foot to it, then you're probably hearing the subdivision of the beat.
(2) The slowest tempo you're like to hear will be around 48 beats per minute.
(3) (a)   The tempo of a slow romantic popular song is usually between 72 and 84 beats per minute.
    (b)   Most disco numbers usually have a tempo between 120 and 132 beats per minute. Anything faster than 132 is difficult to "disco to" because of the intricate dance steps involved.
    (c)   The tempo of the fast section of an orchestral composition may range from about 120 to 180 beats per minute.
    (d)   The tempo of a fast rock song tends to range between 130 and 150 beats per minute. Dancing to rock music is much less formalized and the footwork less important than simply shaking your body; so faster tempos are possible than with disco music.

Now let's return for a moment to our discussion of beats per measure and see how that relates to tempo. Suppose you had to decide the number of beats per measure in this example:

You could give it either three beats or just one beat per measure. If you gave it three beats per measure, you would have to let ♪ = one beat. In that case you would have 3 x 96 or 288 beats in one minute. That's more than four beats per second! As a general rule, 3 beats per second (180 beats per minute) is about the fastest doable tempo.

Examine the two following examples and notice the metronome indications. How many beats per measure would be appropriate for each of these examples? What kind of note should equal one beat?

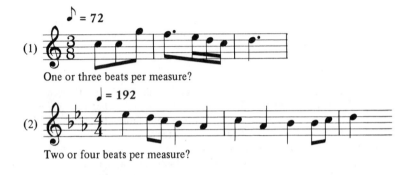

One or three beats per measure?

Two or four beats per measure?

– – – – – – – – – – – – – –

(1) Three beats; an eighth note should equal one beat. One beat per measure would result in only 24 beats per minute.
(2) Two beats; a half note should equal one beat. If you let a quarter equal one beat, then you'd have 192 beats per minute. (Try tapping your foot that fast!)

Asymmetric Meter

Asymmetric meter is meter that has a time signature in which the top number is *not* divisible by 2 or 3. Because of our tendency to hear pulses as though they were in groups of twos or threes, asymmetric meters of five or seven beats (or subdivisions of the beat—or other quantities not divisible by 2 or 3) are heard as combinations of duple and triple meters. For example, $\frac{5}{8}$ is heard as three beats + two beats ♩♩♩♩♩ or two beats + three beats ♩♩♩♩♩ .

In fast tempo the beat may actually change its duration, since each beat may have a different number of *pulses* (the notes in this example represent pulses, not beats):

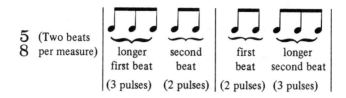

$\dfrac{5}{8}$ (Two beats per measure)

Here's an example of asymmetrical time. Notice that there are two beats per measure.
(1) Which beat is longer? The first or second?
(2) How many pulses per measure?

♩ = 138

First beat second beat First beat second beat

----

(1) The second beat is longer. The first beat = ♩ ; the second = ♩. .
(2) There are five pulses per measure. Notice that the top number in the time signature shows the number of pulses in this example.

1 2 3 4 5

Accents

Certain beats naturally tend to be accented (made stronger) in certain meters. When there are three beats per measure, the first beat of the measure is usually stronger (accented). We'll show this using boxes here:

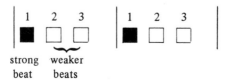

strong   weaker
beat   beats

If there are four beats per measure the first and third tend to be accented.

With six beats per measure we *usually* find the first and fourth beats accented.

Syncopation

Syncopation refers to the shifting of an expected accent, moving it from the usual strong beat to a beat that is usually weak. Notice in the diagram below how we shift the accents in the second measure from the first and third beats to the second and fourth beats.

Application   (expected)   (syncopated)

Try this on a set of bongo drums (if you can lay your hands on them) or any suitable surfaces for beating on (like pots and pans).

—Let each hand be assigned to one drum (or striking area).

—Starting with your *right* hand, begin beating the drums in $\frac{4}{4}$ time with four beats per measure. Alternate your hands so that your right hand always strikes its drum on beats one and three and your left hand strikes its drum on two and four.

—Accent beats one and three like this.

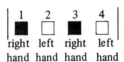

right   left   right   left
hand   hand   hand   hand

—Count out the beats as you strike the drums, saying the numbers one and three clearly.

Do this for several measures until you get the swing of it.

Now let's try some syncopation. First do a measure with the usual accents. Then shift the accents to beats two and four. Then go immediately back to the usual accent. Follow along on this diagram as you perform.

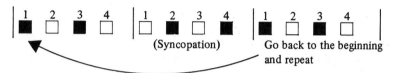

Keep repeating the pattern. Start with *lento* (a slow, easy pace) and work up to *allegro* (a running speed).

Let's return to our discussion of accents for just a moment so you can better understand the other ways that they can be produced.

You notice an accent in music whenever something is *highlighted*. This highlighting can be done by playing a single tone louder than others. This can be indicated in musical notation with the symbol ➤ which is placed directly above or below the notehead:

But an accent is also heard whenever a new musical tone occurs (or a previous tone is repeated). For example, in the first full measure below the listener hears an accent on the first beat simply because a new musical tone starts on beat one. But the listener does not hear an accent on beat three since there is no new musical tone.

In the second measure, however, the listener hears an accent on beats one and three because of the musical tones that start on these beats.

Accents can also be produced by holding certain notes longer than others. These are called *agogic accents*. For example, the first beat of each of these measures is accented because of the half note that starts on the first beat.

One of the common methods of shifting the accent to produce a syncopation is to place a long note-value on the *weak* beat and hold it over into the strong beat so that there is no new musical tone starting on the normally accented beat. In notation, ties are used to hold a note over the bar line.

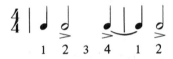

The effect is to make the listener and performer respond physically to provide the missing accent.

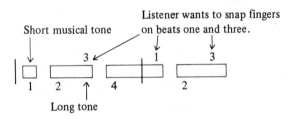

In the previous example notice that no new tone is starting on the beat three in the first measure. In the second measure no new tone starts on the first or third beats. In the example below syncopation occurs in measure one on the tied quarter note and in measure three on the half note.

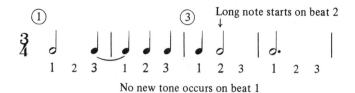

Long note starts on beat 2

No new tone occurs on beat 1

Other methods of shifting the accent are using rests on the strong beats:

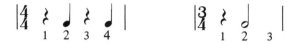

or placing an accent mark (>) on the weak beat:

When performers see the accent marks, they know that they are to accent the notes indicated by playing them suddenly louder than the other notes.

Syncopation Within the Beat

Every beat can be subdivided into two parts, a downbeat and an upbeat. When you tap your foot, it first goes down and then up—thus, the upbeat and downbeat. Syncopation also can involve a shift of weight *within* the beat, from the strong part (downbeat) to the weak part (upbeat). In simple time this is a shift of the natural accent from the first subdivision to the second one—to the "and" part of the beat:

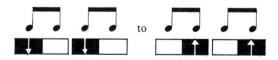

The accented upbeat conflicts with the natural accent of the meter's basic pulse and produces one kind of rhythmic tension.

Application

Tap your foot steadily and slowly (about seventy-two beats per minute). Notice the two distinct movements of your foot as you tap out the beat:

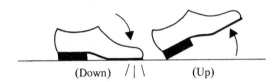

(Down) / | \ (Up)

Next, as you keep tapping your foot, count out several measures of $\frac{2}{4}$ time letting ♩ = one beat. Coordinate your counting and foot tapping so that your foot hits the floor simultaneously with each count.

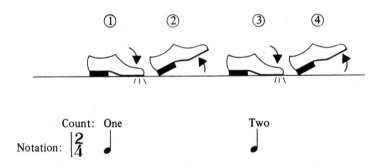

Count: One   Two

Notation: $\frac{2}{4}$ ♩   ♩

Now count out both parts of each beat—that is, count out the downbeat and the upbeat. To do this, you merely say the number of the beat as your foot hits the floor. Then you say "and" as it starts to move up. Say the numbers louder than the "and" since the downbeat is normally accented.

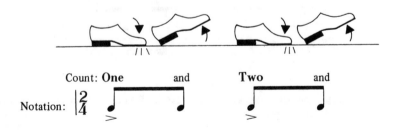

Count: **One**   and   **Two**   and

Notation: $\frac{2}{4}$

Notice that "one" and "two" are printed in bold letters to remind you to accent them. Also notice that the sound produced by your foot hitting the floor helps to accent the downbeats.

Now let's try some syncopation within the beat. Tap and count out the downbeats and upbeats in a similar way, but this time accent the upbeats. Do this by saying the "ands" more loudly than the numbers:

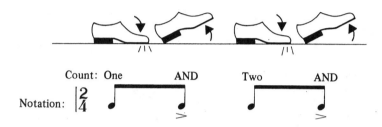

Once you have the feel of this, try snapping your fingers on the upbeat as you continue to tap your foot. This will make the syncopation even more pronounced.

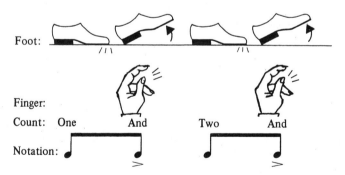

Syncopation adds a special flavor to music: a feeling of energy, drive, excitement. Without any syncopation music tends to sound formal, dignified, or perhaps stiff and old-fashioned. Traditional church music, for example, usually does not make much use of syncopation.

Which of these kinds of music do you think makes heavy use of syncopation?

(1) Dixieland jazz
(2) A funeral march
(3) Rock 'n' roll

— — — — — — — — — — — — — —

(1) and (3): Syncopation is a key distinguishing feature of jazz. Most rock 'n' roll also makes heavy use of syncopation.

Syncopation within the beat occurs in "Evergreen" (Love Theme from *A Star is Born*) by Barbra Streisand:

Notice that the second note coincides with the *upbeat* of the second beat (the "&" of the second beat).

Also, notice that the second tone is tied so that it extends into the third beat. Since no new tone occurs on this normally accented beat, a syncopation occurs; the accent has been shifted to the upbeat of the second beat.

Here are the first four measures from "Evergreen" by Barbra Streisand. There are two syncopations here. We've marked one of them. See if you can find the other.

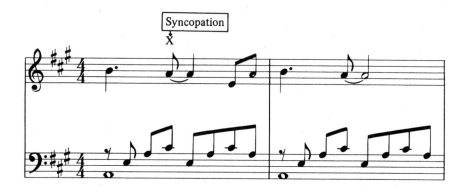

Here is the answer:

Sing the syncopated rhythms below on a pitch of your choice using the syllable "ta." As you do, tap the beat with your foot.

(1)

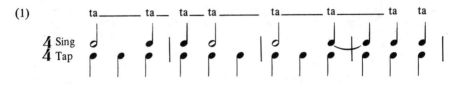

(2)

Put an *X* over each note that shows syncopation in the previous exercise.

– – – – – – – – – – – – – –

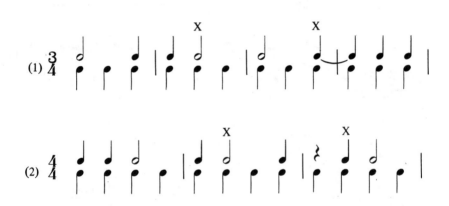

(1) 3/4

(2) 4/4

Put an *X* over each note in this example that shows a syncopation. Remember, in **6/8** time when ♪ = one beat, beats one and four are *usually* accented.

No syncopation here
since rest occurs on a
weak pulse

The first note in measure one would normally be accented; the written accent just makes the natural accent stronger. In measure three the first eighth-note rest coincides with a weak pulse so there is no syncopation. The second rest omits the expected accent on the strong pulse so the natural accent is pushed onto the naturally weak second eighth note of that group:

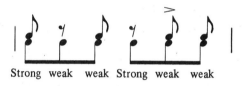

Strong   weak   weak   Strong   weak   weak

Review

In this chapter and the previous one you have learned a good deal about musical time. Let's review the main ideas we've discussed:

- Notes are organized into a hierarchy with each successive note worth half the time value of the previous note.
- Notes can be joined together with ties to make longer time values.
- For every note there is an equivalent rest, which indicates the duration of a silence.
- A dot adds one-half the value of a note to that same note creating a note value *three* times as long as the next smaller note.
- A beat is a regular pulsation indicated by the up-and-down movement of a conductor's hand. You tap your foot to the beat.
- A pulse is a subdivision of a beat. (You feel the pulse, you don't tap your foot to it.)
- Meter refers to the organization of beats into patterns: strong and weak.
- Bar lines divide written music into tiny segments called (aptly) bars or measures.
- The bars help musicians to keep their places and to remember to accent certain notes regularly unless instructed otherwise by special accent marks.

- A time signature indicates the time value of one measure. A time signature of $\frac{3}{4}$ shows that one measure contains three quarter notes or the equivalent in notes and rests.
- A time signature does *not* always show the number of beats per measure (as is sometimes taught by well-meaning music teachers). The number of beats per measure depends largely on the tempo (speed of the beat).
- Tempo is often indicated with Italian terms (since Italian musicians dominated the European musical scene when tempo indications first became popular).
- Different kinds of music have characteristic tempos: rock music (rock 'n' roll) often has a much faster tempo than disco music.
- Syncopation gives music a special life and energy. Syncopation takes place when an accent is shifted so that it does not occur when expected.

In the next chapter we take a break from a discussion of musical time and return to a consideration of musical tones.

CHAPTER FOUR

Scales

Did you ever hear a piece of music and immediately have a good hunch about who composed it, even though you had never heard that specific piece before? Did you ever wonder what gives certain music its distinctive sound? Why does Asian music sound Asian? Why does jazz sound jazzy? What makes some music sound somber or scary, while other music sounds slinky? We can't give you the entire answer in this chapter, but we discuss one of the most important factors: the choice of musical tones that are used in a composition. Similar to the way a chemist can analyze a perfume and specify its ingredients in varying proportions, we can analyze a piece of music and list the musical tones that it comprises. Such a listing in music is called a scale, which is the main focus of this chapter. When you finish this chapter you'll be able to

- Analyze a piece of music and write out the scale that it is based on
- Construct any of these scales starting on any note:
  Major
  Minor
  Chromatic
  Whole tone
- Name the major and minor scales in a special order, known as the "circle of fifths"
- Write out the sharps or flats needed to make the key signature for any major or minor scale
- Indicate what piano keys to use in playing notation that includes a key signature
- Choose from two scales the one that would be more appropriate for creating a specified mood or feeling
- Name scales that are related to any major or minor scale

Scale

A *scale* is simply a list (in musical notation) of the notes used in a piece of music arranged

---

in order according to rising pitches. To see how this works, let's look at an example and derive a scale from it.

The first step in writing out a scale is to decide which note to start with. In most music, one note stands out as a note that gives a feeling of finality, like the last word in a declarative sentence. This note, called the keynote, is used as the first note of the scale. In actual music, the keynote is usually the last note of the piece unless the composer wants to create an unusual effect and leave the listeners "hanging," waiting for an ending that never comes.

So, in building a scale from our example, we start with a G, since it is the last note and it does give us a feeling of finality. (When we come to this note, we get the feeling that this *could* be the end of the composition, if it weren't for the fact that we've only heard eight bars.)

To find the second note for our scale, we look for the next note in the musical alphabet after G. The next note is A, so the first two notes of our scale look like this:

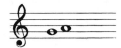

Notice that:

- We are using whole notes to write out the scale, simply because they're more convenient. (We don't have to bother with the stems.)
- We write g′

. . .rather than g″.

In writing out scales, we place the notes close together in a convenient location on the staff regardless of their actual positions on the staff in the music.

Altogether, there are just five notes in the scale that we are constructing. Look back at the musical example on the previous page. See if you can finish that scale by writing in the three remaining notes. *In doing this, don't repeat any notes that have the same name.* For example, if you find two D's, just write one D in the scale.

— — — — — — — — — — — — — — — —

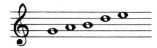

NOTE: We did not include a″

in our scale since we already have a′

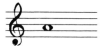

as the second note of the scale.

Let's try another one. Write out a scale for this example Start the scale on c′.

- - - - - - - - - - - - - - -

Pentatonic Scales

Both of the scales in the previous examples are five-note scales. They are called *pentatonic* (penta meaning five and tonic meaning tone). We discuss pentatonic scales in more detail later. Before we can do so, you need to know a little about intervals.

Intervals

An *interval* is the distance between two notes. To understand scales better, it's important for you to know these two intervals: the half step and the whole step.

Half step

The interval between any two adjacent tones is a half step, the smallest interval normally used in Western music. On the keyboard, the half-step interval occurs between any one key and the next adjacent key (white or black).

half step:

White key
to adjacent
black key

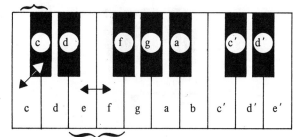

half step:

White key
to adjacent
white key

Whole Step

After the half step, the next smallest interval is the *whole step* or *whole tone*. It consists of two half steps.

On the keyboard you move a whole step by skipping over one key, whether black or white. You may move a whole step by:

—skipping from a white key to a black key

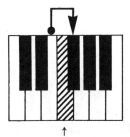

↑
You should skip over this key.

—skipping from a white to a white key (over a black)

You should skip over this key

—skipping from a black key to a black key (over a white)

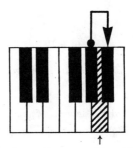

You skip over this key.

Tell whether each of these intervals is a half or whole step. (Abbreviate H for half and W for whole step).

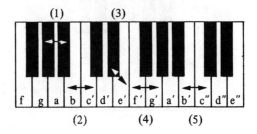

– – – – – – – – – – – – – – – –

(1) W (2) H (3) H (4) W (5) H

Notice that half steps always occur between the notes E and F and between B and C. The distance between any other adjacent letters of the musical alphabet are *whole steps*. Keeping this in mind, label each interval below as either a half or whole step.

– – – – – – – – – – – – – – – –

(1) H (E to F is always a half step)
(2) H (B to C is always a half step)
(3) W

Diatonic Scales

Now that you understand half and whole steps, we can go into more detail about scales. One of the most common types of scales in music is the *diatonic* scale. Originally a diatonic scale was one that contained all seven letters of the musical alphabet (C, D, E, F, G, A, B) with no sharps or flats (the tones that correspond today to the white keys of the piano).

If you start with the note C and play all of the notes up to the next C, you would be playing a diatonic scale:

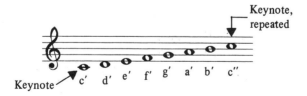

Notice that after writing all seven notes of the scale, we include a repeat of the keynote C. This is usually done with scales because this helps us see the relationship of the seventh note of the scale to the keynote. If we stop on the seventh note of the scale, we are left hanging. By continuing up to the keynote, we make the scale sound complete and get a better feeling for the musical quality of the scale.

There are seven different kinds of diatonic scales, each with its own name and musical quality. Sometimes the word *mode* is used when referring to these diatonic scales. The particular quality of each diatonic scale (or mode) is determined by the *keynote* that is used. That's because with different keynotes, the half steps and whole steps occur in different places. The next exercise will make this clear.

(1) Examine the diatonic scales below and mark the location of the half steps as we have done with the Ionian scale.

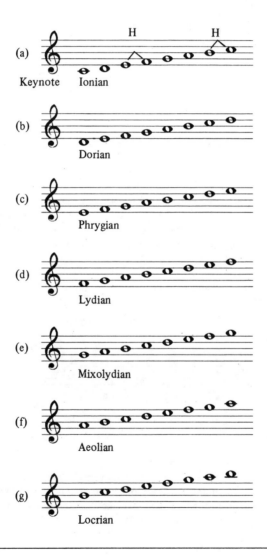

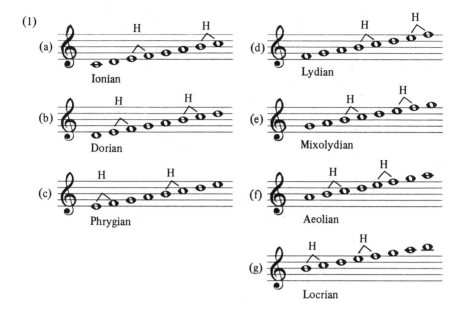

(2) Which scales have a half step between the seventh and eighth tones?
(3) Which have a half step between the fifth and sixth tones?

— — — — — — — — — — — — — — — —

(2) The Ionian and Lydian scales have half steps between the seventh and eighth tones.
(3) The Aeolian and Phrygian scales have half steps between the fifth and sixth tones.

Major and Minor Scales

During the seventeenth, eighteenth, and nineteenth centuries, the most popular diatonic scales in Western music were the Ionian and Aeolian modes. The Ionian mode came to be known as the major scale, and the Aeolian mode the minor scale. Since major and minor scales are still used quite frequently today, let's examine them in more detail.

Major Scale

Originally, the major scale (the Ionian mode) always had C as its keynote, and only white keys on the piano were needed when this scale was used. But later, musicians began to use different pitches for the keynote while keeping the same pattern of whole steps and half steps as that used in the major scale beginning with C. As you will recall, the Ionian mode (major scale) has half steps in these locations:

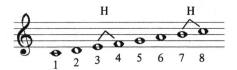

Notice that there are half steps between tones three and four and between tones seven and eight.

Now suppose we begin a scale on G instead of C.

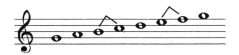

As is, this is a Mixolydian rather than an Ionian (or major) scale. To transform it into a major scale, we need to raise the seventh tone of the scale so that there is a half step between tones seven and eight.

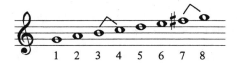

Notice that with the change from F to F#, we have a major scale with G as the keynote, called a G-major scale. Music composed with the tones of this scale is said to be in the key of G-major.

In experimenting with different keynotes, musicians noticed that if they used the fifth note of an existing scale for the keynote of a *new* scale, they only had to raise the *seventh* tone of the scale to make the half steps occur in the same places. Notice that's what we just did. We started with a major scale built on c′:

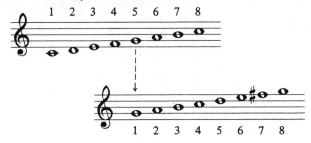

...then we built a new scale on g′ and *raised* the seventh tone of the new scale.

Now, let's take the fifth tone of the G-major scale and build a new scale on it:

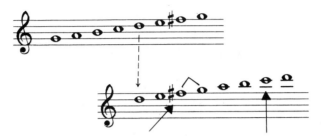

Notice that we keep the F♯" from the G scale: This gives us the needed half step between 3 and 4.

Here we need to change something to get a half step between the 7th and 8th steps.

In the example above, add a sharp to the seventh degree of the scale so that a half step occurs between tones seven and eight.

_ _ _ _ _ _ _ _ _ _ _ _ _ _ _

Let's write another major scale to be sure you've got the idea. Take the fifth tone of the D-major scale and use that as the keynote for a new scale. Remember the rule: keep the accidentals and raise the seventh tone.

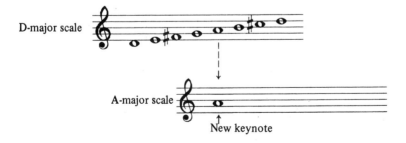

D-major scale

A-major scale

New keynote

A-major scale

More on Building Major Scales

Just as the early musicians discovered that they could easily make new scales by moving *up* five notes, they discovered that they could do the same by moving *down* five notes.

To make a *new* scale by counting down, you start with the eighth note of the old scale (which is the same as the keynote) and count down five notes. This is called counting down a fifth. (Note that you consider the keynote "1" as you count from one to five.)

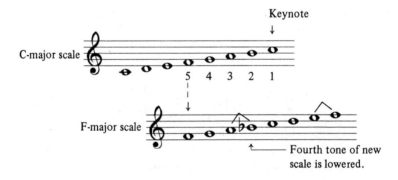

After counting down a fifth, you use the note you land on as the keynote for a new scale. To make the required half step between the third and fourth tones of the scale, you lower the fourth tone of the new scale. Note that in this method too, the new scale has only *one* tone that is not in the set of tones used in the old scale. Since there is only one tone that is different, these two scales are said to be *related*.

Now you try it. Here is an F-major scale. Use the "count down a fifth" procedure to create a new related scale that has only one new tone.

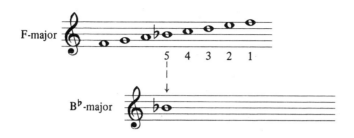

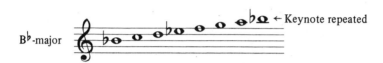

Notice that the fourth tone of the new scale is lowered. This is the only tone that is not in the old scale.

You may wonder why we always count up or down a fifth to create a new scale. We do this simply because it's easy. To make the new scale all you do is change one note.

(1) When moving the keynote up a fifth, you *raise* the _____ tone of the original scale. (Which one?)

(2) When moving the keynote down a fifth, you lower the _____ tone of the original scale. (Which one?)

- - - - - - - - - - - - - - -

(1) seventh   (2) fourth

The Circle of Fifths

If we start with the scale of C-major and keep building new scale by going up a fifth, we can identify *all* of the scales (or keys) that use sharps. Similarly, we can identify all of the keys (scales) that use flats by going *down* a fifth.

- The sharp keys are: G, D, A, E, B, F♯, C♯
- The flat keys are: F, B♭, E♭, A♭, D♭, G♭, C♭

Often these keys are written around a circle to show how the sharp keys and flat keys eventually meet and overlap. This is called the circle of fifths.

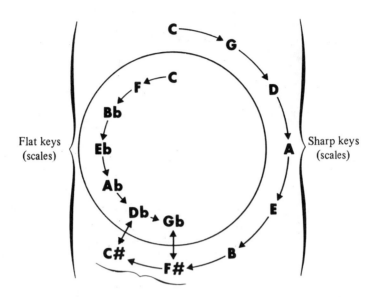

Note that the key of C♯ is actually the same key as D♭ and the key of F♯ is the same as G♭. These keys are said to be *enharmonic* equivalents.

Modulation and the Circle of Fifths

A modulation is simply a change of keynote (called change of key for short). Often composers will *modulate* to a new key in the middle of a piece of music to provide variety. Somehow the same music played in a new key seems to have a fresh sound.

So that the change of key doesn't sound too harsh, composers often modulate to a related key, that is, a key that uses no more than one new tone. An easy way to find a related key is to look at an adjacent key on the circle of fifths. For example, if you are using the scale of A and you wanted to modulate to a new key, you could easily modulate to the scale of D or to the scale of E.

(1) Suppose you are using the scale of C♯. What two related scales could you modulate to, each of which would have only one tone different from the original scale of C♯? (Hint: Refer to the circle of fifths and remember the scale of C♯-major is equivalent to the scale of D♭-major).

(2) True or false: The G–major scale is higher in pitch than the C-major scale? True _____   False _____

— — — — — — — — — — — — — — — — —

(1) You could modulate to A♭-major or to F♯-major. (In modulating to A♭-major, you

first need to imagine that you are in the scale of D♭-major instead of C♯).

(2) False. Any G-major scale could be higher or lower than most any C-major scale depending on which G or C each scale started on. The G-major scale starting on g′ would be *higher* than the C-major scale starting on c′. But the G-major scale starting on G would be *lower*.

Key Signatures for the Major Scales

We have seen how all the major scales, other than C-major, contain different numbers of sharps or flats. Instead of having to write a sharp or flat every time, a shorthand method makes this automatic by collecting all the different sharps or flats in a scale and arranging them in a fixed order and location at the beginning of each line of music immediately after the clef sign. This collection is the *key signature*. It provides for the automatic raising or lowering of tones throughout an entire line of music.

Without a key signature, notes might look like this:

With a key signature, the notes would look like this:

When an accidental (sharp or flat sign) appears in the key signature, it affects every note that has the same letter name as the line or space that it occupies.

This sharp sign on f″ means that all F notes are sharped, not just f″.

If the key signature has an F♯ and you want to write F♮, then you must put a natural sign before the F note:

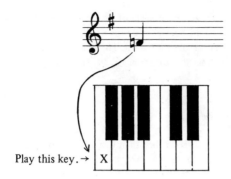

Play this key. →

Once the natural sign is placed in front of a note, then that note stays natural for an entire measure.

One measure

These notes are f′♮

After a barline, all sharps (or flats) in the key signature are automatically reinstated.

bar line   No sharp needed, this note is f′♯!

This next example illustrates the rules we've just discussed. Each note is numbered. On the keyboard below, the numbers show which keys would be used to play those notes.

Table 4-1

Note Number	Comments
1	In the key signature, there is a flat on a'. This automatically flattens *all* A notes, so we also flatten a''.
2	The natural sign is needed here if the composer wants E-natural, since E-flat appears in the key signature.
4	The natural sign applied to note two also affects note four.
6	The bar line reinstated the key signature; therefore, we play e''-flat.

Now, you try it. What piano key would you use to play each of these notes? Number the keys as we did in the previous example.

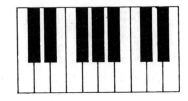

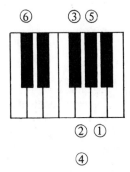

Using Key Signatures

Beginning music students often have trouble with key signatures, especially those that contain three or more sharps or flats. The secret is to "think in the scale," rather than to try to remember each sharp or flat individually. When we say "think in the scale," we mean have a clear image of the set of tones in the scale. Even if you don't play a keyboard instrument, it's helpful to visualize the keys on the keyboard.

So when you see the key signature for the key (scale) of E:

. . .you visualize this:

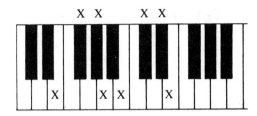

The idea is to perceive the scale as a whole, rather than as a series of sharps, naturals, or flats.

Optional Exercise

On a keyboard, each scale also has a definite feel or shape. If you have access to a keyboard, try this:

(1) Put your hands on a keyboard as shown here so that you are feeling the scale of E-major.

(2) Close your eyes and pay attention to the shape of the scale: how certain fingers are up higher (on black keys) and others are down lower (on white keys).

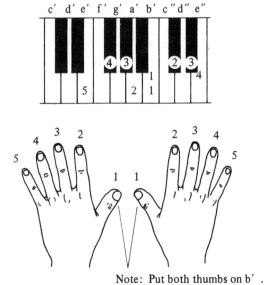

Note: Put both thumbs on b′ .

- Left hand:
   little finger (5th) on e′
   4th finger on f′♯
   3rd finger on g′♯
   2nd finger on a′
   thumb on b′

- Right hand:
   thumb on b′
   2nd finger on c″♯
   3rd finger on d″♯
   4th finger on e″

(3) Now with your eyes still closed, take your hands away from the keyboard a moment. Then put them back quickly.

(4) Open your eyes, check your hand position. Correct any errors in the placement of your fingers.

When you can do this exercise quickly with accuracy, then you will have a better idea of what we mean by "thinking in the scale."

Remembering Key Signatures

It's important to be able to look at the key signature at the beginning of a piece of music and be able to tell the keynote and scale that is being used. Once musicians know this they are better able to

- Remember which tones to use and which to avoid
- Anticipate which tones will likely come next
- Improvise music that fits with the written music

Major Key Signatures

If sharps are used in a major key signature, the keynote is the note directly above the last sharp:

Last sharp is C♯, so the keynote is D. Therefore, this is the key signature for the scale of D-major.

Assuming that each of these is the key signature for a major key, what is the name of the major scale?

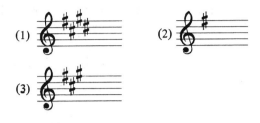

- - - - - - - - - - - - - - - -

(1) E-major   (2) G-major   (3) A-major

Placement of Sharps in Key Signature

In key signatures, the sharps are *always* placed in this order and in these locations:

G-clef

F-clef

Which of these key signatures is OK? What's wrong with the incorrect ones?

- - - - - - - - - - - - - - -

The correct one is (3). Example (1) is wrong because the first sharp should be f″♯, not f′♯. In example (2) the third sharp should be g′♯, not g′♯.

It's useful to memorize the order and placement of the sharps, because once you do, you can easily write the key signature for any scale (key) using sharps. The order, again, is

F–C–G–D–A–E–B. (See the proper placement of these sharps above.)

All you do is recite the sharps in order until you come to the letter preceding the keynote in the musical alphabet. For example, suppose you want to know the key signature for the key of E-major. Since D precedes E in the musical alphabet, all you do is recite the sharps in order until you come to D: F–C–G–D.

What are the letter names of the sharps for the key of B-major?

_ _ _ _ _ _ _ _ _ _ _ _ _ _

F–C–G–D–A. Notice that the last sharp is the letter preceding the keynote (B) in the musical alphabet.

Try another one. What are the sharps for the key of A? (Remember, G precedes A in the musical alphabet.)

_ _ _ _ _ _ _ _ _ _ _ _ _ _

F–C–G

Placement of Flats in a Key Signature

Now that you've learned the key signatures for the sharp keys, let's consider the flat keys.

F major (1♭)   B♭ major (2♭)   E♭ major (3♭)   A♭ major (4♭)

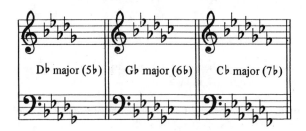

D♭ major (5♭)   G♭ major (6♭)   C♭ major (7♭)

The pattern for adding flats alternates one flat above and one below.

The sequence of flats used in the flat keys proceeds in descending fifths B-E-A-D-G-C-F. It is useful to memorize the series of flats and the way they appear in the signature.

Notice the pattern of placement of flats in the key signature: up, down, up, down. Also notice the first four flats spell the word "bead."

Any other placement of flats in the signature is wrong and confusing to experienced musicians.

By placing the flats in the exact same *place* in key signatures, composers make it easy for musicians to tell at a glance what scale (or key) is being used.

By putting the flats in the same *order*, you make it easier for yourself to recall what flats are needed for specific scales. *A valuable rule here is that the next to the last flat in a key signature tells the name of the flat key.*

If these flats are used:
   B E A D
...the key is A♭ since the next to the last flat is A.

B E Ⓐ D
       ↗
Next to the last flat.

Suppose you have these flats in the key signature:

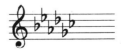

(1) What is the next to the last flat?
(2) What is the major scale that this key signature indicates?

– – – – – – – – – – – – – – –

(1) G   (2) The scale of G♭-major.

Now, on this staff write the key signature for the key (or scale) of E♭-major. (Hint: Recite the flats in order until you come to E♭, then say one more flat and you'll have it).

– – – – – – – – – – – – – – –

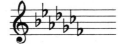

Try one more. What major key is this the key signature for?

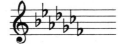

– – – – – – – – – – – – – – –

C♭-major

Now that you can write the key signature for any major key and you can name all of the major keys by using the circle of fifths diagram, let's consider the other widely used diatonic scale: the minor scale.

Minor Scales

As we mentioned earlier, the minor scale is really the same as the Aeolian scale. Sometimes there are slight variations to the minor scale. When there are no variations, the scale is called *natural* minor. The two variations are called *harmonic* and *melodic* minor.

Here is the natural minor scale along with its two variations.

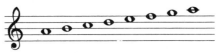

Natural minor (same as Aeolian mode)

Harmonic minor

Melodic minor

The melodic minor has two versions: one for ascending, one for descending notes.

(1) Between which scale tones do half steps occur in each ascending version of the minor scale?
(2) Which tone of the scale is raised to produce the harmonic minor?
(3) Which tones are raised to produce the ascending melodic minor?
(4) The descending version of the melodic minor is the same as which other scale?

— — — — — — — — — — — — — —

(1) Natural: between two and three and between five and six; Harmonic: between two and three, between five and six, between seven and eight. Melodic: between two and three, and between seven and eight.
(2) Seventh
(3) Sixth and seventh
(4) Natural minor

Building Natural Minor Scales

We can build natural minor scales in the same way as we did major scales. For example, we can use the fifth tone of the A-minor scale to build a new related scale on E:

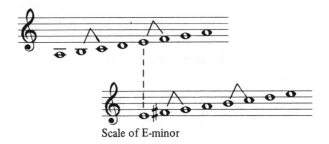

Scale of E-minor

Notice that we need to raise the second tone to provide a half step between the second and third tones.

Similarly we can count *down* a fifth to build another related key:

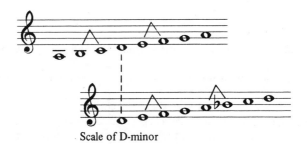

Scale of D-minor

Sixth tone is *lowered* to provide half step between tones five and six.

(1) What two minor scales are related to E-minor?
(2) Using the fifth tone of E-minor as a keynote, write out one of these related keys. Don't forget to make the change needed to provide the half step between the second and third tones.

- - - - - - - - - - - - - -

(1) B-minor (up a fifth); A-minor (down a fifth)

(2)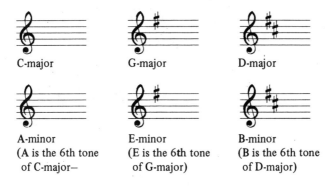

Key Signatures for the Minor Scales

The natural minor scales, like the major scales, have key signatures which contain all the sharps or flats needed for the scale. Here are the key signatures for three major scales and three minor scales:

C-major	G-major	D-major

A-minor
(A is the 6th tone
of C-major—

E-minor
(E is the 6th tone
of G-major)

B-minor
(B is the 6th tone
of D-major)

Notice that

- C-major has the same key signature as A-minor.
- G-major has the same key signature as E-minor.
- D-major has the same key signature as B-minor.

Based on this pattern, which minor scale has the same key signature as F-major?

- - - - - - - - - - - - - -

D (natural)-minor. D is the sixth tone of F-major.

Relative Major and Minor Scales

As you learned in the previous question, there is a definite relationship between the key signatures of the major and minor scales. As a rule of thumb, the sixth tone of a major scale can be used as the keynote of a natural minor scale. That minor scale will have the same key signature as the major scale. The minor key is called the *relative minor* of the major key. (The major key is called the relative major of the minor key).

This minor key is called *relative* because it contains the *same tones* as the major key; the only difference is that the two scales have different keynotes. For this reason, it's easy to modulate from a major key to its relative minor (or *to* a relative major key *from* a minor key). Such modulations are especially effective because they can be smoothly executed (due to the common tones), and the change from major to minor (or vice versa) provides an interesting change in the musical effect.

A good example of this is the American folk song "The Erie Canal," which begins in the key of D-minor.

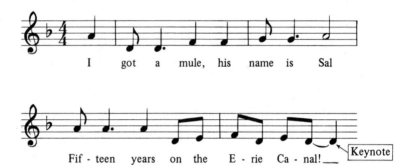

But the refrain of the same song uses the relative major.

What key does the refrain use?

F-major. You can tell this because the F note at the end of the example gives a feeling of finality, since this is the keynote. Also, the key of F-major has one flat, as in the example. Another way to figure it out is to think: D is the sixth tone of what major scale?

Other Diatonic Modes (Scales)

Because the Ionian (major) and Aeolian (minor) modes were the most widely used during the past three centuries, many music books focus almost exclusively on these modes. Since the late nineteenth century, however, musicians have been returning to ancient modes as a way of giving their music a fresh "new" sound. Often a modern-day composer will use the ancient modes for just a few measures and then return to either the major or minor modes. In the next example, John Lennon and Paul McCartney use one of the ancient modes in "Eleanor Rigby" to give it a distinctive, "new" sound.

Keynote

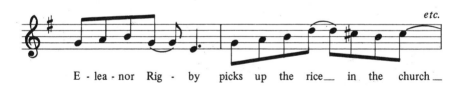

E - lea - nor Rig - by   picks   up   the   rice___   in   the   church ___

If we write out a scale for this song, it would look like this:

← Keynote repeated

Using the information on pages 76 through 77, see if you can determine which mode is being used.

— — — — — — — — — — — — —

The Dorian mode. We know this because the Dorian mode is the only one with half steps between tones two and three and tones six and seven.

Now try the same with the following musical excerpt.

(1) Write out the scale used to compose this excerpt from "Hello, Goodbye" by John Lennon and Paul McCartney.
(2) Mark the location of the half steps.
(3) Between which tones do the half steps occur?
(4) Refer to pages 76 through 77 and identify the name of the mode being used.

— — — — — — — — — — — — —

(1), (2)

(3) The half steps are between tones three and four and tones six and seven.
(4) Mixolydian (the only mode with half steps between tones three and four and tones six and seven).

OTHER SCALES

Although the diatonic scales predominate, there are several other scales. Two important ones are the whole tone scale and the chromatic scale.

The Whole Tone Scale

A *whole tone* scale consists of six tones, each separated by a whole step. Because the whole tone scale has no half steps, it seems to lack direction. (A half step in a scale helps to give a sense of arrival. For example, in the major scale, when the seventh tone progresses up to the keynote by a half step, the keynote is strengthened. That's why the minor scale is sometimes altered to the harmonic minor scale in which there is a half step between tones seven and eight).

When a composer wants to create a feeling of being lost or a dream-like effect, the whole tone scale comes in handy.

There are only two whole tone scales. One uses these notes:

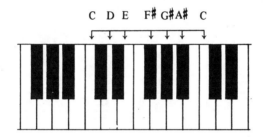

... the other uses these:

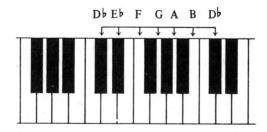

The Chromatic Scale

The *chromatic* scale is a scale of twelve different notes with a half step between each note. Sometimes the chromatic scale is referred to as the twelve-tone scale. When writing the ascending version of the twelve-tone scale, it is customary to sharpen every other note; when writing the descending version, to flatten every other note.

Here is the first part of the chromatic scale beginning on A.

(1) Complete the ascending twelve-tone scale be adding seven additional notes.
(2) Why do we write out the scale with thirteen notes when it's called a twelve-tone scale?
(3) Are there any pitch names within the octave that are *not* used in the chromatic scale?

Notice that we wrote B♯ instead of C♮, since it's customary to use a sharp when necessary on other notes.

— — — — — — — — — — — — — —

(1)

Be sure you wrote E♯ and not F.

(2) We write thirteen notes because we customarily repeat the keynote to show the relationship of the last note of the scale to the keynote (as in the diatonic scale).
(3) No. The chromatic scale includes every possible pitch name within the octave.

Some composers like to use every one of the twelve notes of the chromatic scale before returning to a note that has been previously used. In this way, there is no one note that can be thought of as the keynote, since no one tone predominates. This music (often called twelve-tone music) seems to have a restless, scary sound.

Here are two examples.

(1) Which one would be called twelve-tone music? (Write out the scale if you need to.)
(2) Which would probably be more appropriate as background music for a tense scene in a science fiction movie?

(a)

(b)

- - - - - - - - - - - - - - - -

(1) Example (b)
(2) Example (b). Example (a) is actually based on a pentatonic (five-tone) scale. You may have noticed the syncopation in measures 3 and 4 of example (b). This would also contribute to the restless, scary effect produced by the twelve-tone music.

For each of the following examples:

(1) Write out the scale that the example is based on.
(2) Mark the location of the half steps.
(3) Name the scale that is used.

(a)

Scale for Example (a)

(Begin with d')   Name of scale: _____

(b)

Scale for Example (b)

(Begin with c′)   Name of scale: _____

– – – – – – – – – – – – – – – – –

(a)

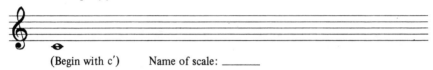

Chromatic scale

(b)

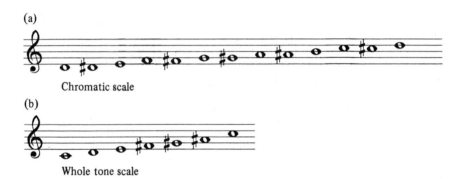

Whole tone scale

Review

You've learned a lot of different pieces of information about scales and keys. Let's review the main ideas and then pull a few things together. A scale, as you've seen, is a systematic ordering of all the notes used in a piece of music. The tones ordered according to rising pitches. The first note ordered is the keynote—the note that gives a feeling of finality in the piece of music. Although we said that all tones are ordered, we need to qualify that. We notate the tones which have different pitch names. But if a piece contains, say, E♭ and e♭ and e″b, we still represent E♭ only once in the scale. E♭ is considered basically the same note as e♭; they're just in different octaves.

As you have probably noticed, the terms *scale* and *key* are often used interchangeably. One difference: when we use *key*, we are talking about either a minor or major scale; *scale*, however, can refer to any of many different kinds of scales. There are many kinds of scales. We have looked at these: Ionian (major), Dorian, Phrygian, Lydian, Myxolydian, Aeolian (minor), whole tone, pentatonic, twelve-tone.

Scales are derived from music. We examine a piece and systematically list the tones that have been used. But the reverse is also true. Musicians often decide in advance that they are going to play or compose in a certain scale because they like the flavor of that scale.

The distinctive quality of a scale results from the intervals between the different scale steps. A major scale sounds like a major scale because there are always half-steps between tones three and four and tones seven and eight, whole steps everywhere else. As you can see, intervals are crucial to understanding what makes music work. In the next chapter, you will learn more about intervals.

CHAPTER FIVE

Intervals

In the last chapter you learned how to construct the same kind of scale on various key-notes. You did this by putting the proper kind of *interval* between the various tones of the scale. In building a major scale you used these intervals:

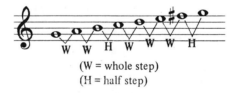

(W = whole step)
(H = half step)

In studying music it's also useful to examine the interval between other tones of the scale. Part of the distinctive sound of the Mixolydian scale for example, results from what is called the *minor seventh* interval which occurs between the keynote and the seventh tone of the scale.

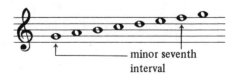

minor seventh
interval

A knowledge of intervals is important in developing a better understanding of the various scales. There are many other good reasons for learning about intervals. Intervals are like building blocks: not only can you build scales with them, but you can analyze and build *chords* (combinations of tones that sound simultaneously). As you'll see shortly, a knowledge of intervals can be a big help in learning to read music.

When you complete this chapter, you will be able to

- Differentiate between melodic intervals and harmonic intervals
- Identify the intervals of the major scale
- Identify the "perfect" and "major" intervals of the major scale
- Recognize perfect, major, minor, diminished, or augmented intervals in musical notation
- Notate major, minor, augmented, and diminished intervals from a given pitch
- Give the abbreviations for each of the intervals (for example, "P5" for "perfect fifth")
- Identify the common "compound intervals"
- Invert given intervals
- Use a knowledge of intervals to read notes on ledger lines
- Recognize the intervals in familiar songs

MELODIC AND HARMONIC INTERVALS

When pitches sound at different times, they form a melodic interval. Melody refers to the upward and downward movement of a series of tones. Usually a melody has a distinctive sound and you can easily recognize it when you hear it.

Here are some examples of melodic intervals:

(half   (minor   (major

step)   seventh)   third)

(You learn how these intervals are named later.)

When two tones sound simultaneously they form an *harmonic interval*. Harmony refers to the simultaneous sounding of tones. In music notation we show that notes are to sound simultaneously by stacking them directly on top of each other like this:

In this example, the note g′ is to sound simultaneously with the note e′.

When two simultaneously sounding notes are right next to each other on the staff (like g′ and a′), the lower notehead is placed on the left side of the stem and the higher notehead on the right side of the stem. The noteheads just barely touch each other. Otherwise the notes will crowd each other too much and be hard to read.

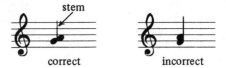

correct   incorrect

Identify the notes in the following examples as forming an harmonic or a melodic interval. Write H or M in each case.

(a)_____ (b)____ (c)_____ (d) _____

- - - - - - - - - - - - - - - - -

(a) M   (b) H   (c) H   (d) M

In (c), although the notes are not stacked directly on top of each other, we can still tell that they are to be sounded together simultaneously because they are touching each other. In (d) the notes are separated by a space so we know the interval is a melodic one.

Recognizing and Naming Intervals

An interval name always has a *numerical* component. Here are some interval names:

Table 5-1

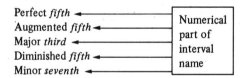

For now, let's focus on how the numerical part of the interval name is determined. Later we explain what is meant by words like "perfect," "augmented," "diminished."

The numerical part of the name of an interval is determined by the number of staff positions (lines and spaces) it includes. The interval in the following example is called a *fifth* because it includes five staff positions (three lines and two spaces):

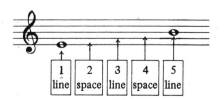

This interval is a *third*:

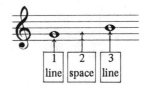

What is the numerical name for this interval?

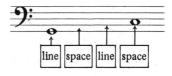

Fourth (*two* lines and *two* spaces: 2 + 2 = 4)

So the numerical part of an interval name is decided by the number of staff positions. Two exceptions to this rule are the cases where there are one or eight staff positions. The first happens when two instruments or voices sound the exact same pitch. Such an interval is called a *unison* (rather than a first). The other interval, eight positions apart is called an *octave*.

In this next example, notice that on the third beat of the measure the violin and oboe are in unison. (Notes with stems up show tones played by the violin; notes with the stems down, the oboe.)

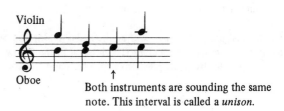

Both instruments are sounding the same note. This interval is called a *unison*.

What is the basic name of each of these intervals?

- -

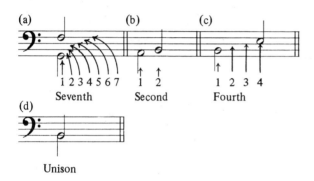

To make it easier to talk about intervals we'd like to introduce another term, *degree*, which means the same as "tone of the scale." Instead of saying "third tone of the scale," we simply say "third degree." Would it be correct to refer to this tone as the fifth degree?

- - - - - - - - - - - - - - - -

Yes. It is the fifth tone of the E-major scale.

Determining the Complete Interval Name

So far we've dealt just with the numerical part of the interval name. Now let's focus on the other part of the names (the part that has words like perfect, augmented, diminished, or minor).

In analyzing an interval it is important to *imagine* that you are in the *major* or *minor* scale of the lower note. Then count upward along this imaginary scale using the lower note *as if it were* a keynote. The degree occupied by the upper tone gives the complete interval name.

In the following examples the intervals are formed by combining each of the degrees of the C-major scale with the *keynote* C. Note how the upper scale degree matches the numerical name of the interval. Also, notice that some intervals are called *perfect* and some *major*.

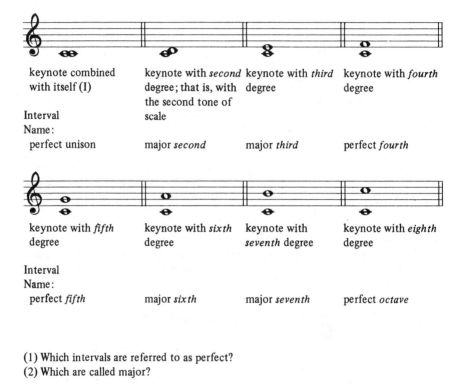

keynote combined with itself (I)

keynote with *second* degree; that is, with the second tone of scale

keynote with *third* degree

keynote with *fourth* degree

Interval Name:

perfect unison   major *second*   major *third*   perfect *fourth*

keynote with *fifth* degree

keynote with *sixth* degree

keynote with *seventh* degree

keynote with *eighth* degree

Interval Name:

perfect *fifth*   major *sixth*   major *seventh*   perfect *octave*

(1) Which intervals are referred to as perfect?
(2) Which are called major?

– – – – – – – – – – – – –

(1) The unison, fourth, fifth, and octave
(2) The second, third, sixth, and seventh

Although early music theorists had reasons for calling some intervals perfect and others major, the reasons are obscure to most musicians today. At one time the unison, octave, fifth, and fourth were considered more agreeable sounding than the other intervals; hence, the term perfect was used. (In German the word *rein*, meaning "clean"' is used for "perfect." To early German theorists these intervals probably had a clean as opposed to a muddy sound.)

Minor, Diminished and Augmented Intervals

We can change an interval by increasing or decreasing its size by a half step. Suppose we have this interval:

(5th)

We can decrease its size by changing it to

or

(Diminished)

Or we can increase its size by changing it to

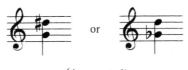

or

(Augmented)

When intervals are changed in size their names are changed in one of these ways: When perfect and major intervals are increased by a half step, they are *augmented*. Perfect intervals that are decreased by a half step are *diminished*. Major intervals that are decreased in size become minor.

This table summarizes this nomenclature.

Table 5-2

Type of interval	Increased by half step	Decreased by half step
major	augmented	minor
perfect	augmented	diminished

Recognizing Increased and Decreased Intervals

It's really difficult for most beginners to recognize increased and decreased intervals. For example, look at this interval:

Would you say this interval has been decreased?

— — — — — — — — — — — — — — —

Yes, it has been decreased. Wonder why we say this? Read on!

Remember, when examining an interval, you must first imagine that the lower note is the keynote of a *major* scale. So when you see:

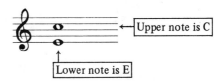

. . .you imagine:

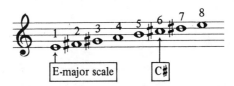

Now, notice that the sixth degree of the E-major scale is C♯. But the upper note of the interval is C♮. Since C♮ is one half step *lower* than C♯, we say the interval has been *decreased*.

Now let's try another one. This gets tricky, so watch closely! Has this interval been increased?

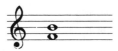

(If you need a hint, drop down to the next line.)

– – – – – – – – – – – – – – –

HINT: Imagine the F-major scale because the lower note of the interval is F.

F-major scale

Notice that the fourth degree is B♭.

– – – – – – – – – – – – – – –

Yes, the interval has been increased, as you can see if you think of the F-major scale. B♭ has been raised by a half step to B♮.

Now, let's practice analyzing and naming some intervals. What's the first thing we do in analyzing this interval?

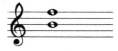

– – – – – – – – – – – – – – –

Imagine a B-major scale because the bottom note of the interval is B.

Notice that:

- The upper note of the interval is F♮.
- When F occurs in the B major scale, it is F♯, not F♮.

Therefore, what do we call this interval? (Refer to Table 5-2 if you need to.)

(a) Perfect fifth
(b) Minor fifth
(c) Diminished fifth

– – – – – – – – – – – – – – – –

(c) Remember fourths and fifths that are decreased in size are called diminished.

Now try naming this one.

– – – – – – – – – – – – – – –

Major third. (The third degree of the A-major scale is C♯. Since the upper note of the interval is also C♯, the interval is neither increased nor decreased. When thirds are neither increased nor decreased, they are major. (See Table 5-2.)

What interval is this?

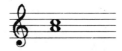

– – – – – – – – – – – – – – –

Minor third. (The C♯ has been lowered to C♮.)

Here are several intervals. Can you name them correctly?

Abbreviate your answers like this: M = major; m = minor; A = augmented; d = diminished; P = perfect.

– – – – – – – – – – – – – –

1. A4	4. d4	7. m6	10. m2
2. P4	5. m7	8. M6	
3. P4	6. M7	9. M6	

(Remember these abbreviations. We will be using them from now on.)

Now, you make some intervals. Add a note directly above this note to create a M7.

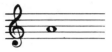

For additional practice, make the following intervals:

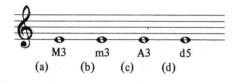

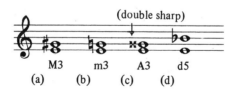

Compound Intervals

So far you've learned about intervals of an octave or smaller. There are also intervals greater than an octave, created by adding intervals above the repeated tone of the octave. For example, a ninth is the same as an octave plus a second, and a tenth is the same as an octave plus a third.

octave	ninth	tenth	eleventh	twelfth
(8ᵛᵉ)	(8ᵛᵉ plus second)	(8ᵛᵉ plus third)	(8ᵛᵉ plus fourth)	(8ᵛᵉ plus fifth)

Because we can think of each of these larger intervals as an octave plus some smaller interval, they are commonly called *compound intervals*. Sometimes a compound interval can have a dramatic effect, as in this:

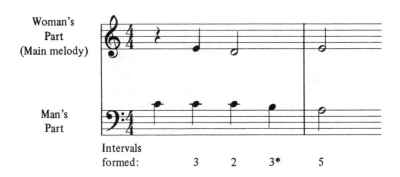

This melody portrays *ascending* by leaping upward. This leap of a ninth is dramatic because the interval is so large

Inversion of Intervals

When two or more instruments or singers perform together, each one may have its own melody. As they sound musical tones together, they produce certain intervals. Suppose a song involves a man and a woman singing together. For the first verse, the woman might sing the main melody and the man a less important melody. They would produce intervals as marked:

Arrangement One

*The interval here is a minor third because the note b (in the man's part) is sounding together with a note d' in the woman's part.

The parts might also be reversed so that the man sings the main melody and the woman sings the less important melody, producing the following intervals:

Arrangement Two

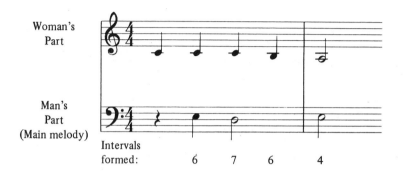

Woman's
Part

Man's
Part
(Main melody)

Intervals
formed: 6   7   6   4

Examine the two arrangements to answer these questions:

(1) How does the man's part (main melody) in Arrangement Two differ from the woman's part (main melody) in Arrangement One?
(2) Are the harmonic intervals in the two arrangements the same or different?
(3) (Optional) Try playing the two arrangements on a keyboard instrument. Which version do you like better?

— — — — — — — — — — — — — — — —

(1) The man's part is an octave lower than the woman's.
(2) Different
(3) We like the first version better. (We'll explain why in a moment.)

Notice that in this exercise a different interval is formed when the top note of an interval (from woman's part of Arrangement One) is moved down an octave (into the man's part of Arrangement Two). Formation of a new interval in this way is called *inversion*. Awareness of the inversion of intervals is important because different intervals seem to work better than others in certain musical styles.

We feel the interval of a fifth in the first version of the previous example sounds right. But in the second version the fifth is inverted to a fourth and to our ears a fourth sounds out-of-place here. Of course, musical tastes differ and you might not agree, but nevertheless it's important to be aware when inversion takes place. Now, let's take a closer look at the inversion process.

If you start with an interval, say, a fifth, and you move the top note down an octave, you get a fourth, as in (a) here:

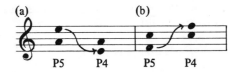

You also get a perfect fourth when you shift the bottom tone of a P5 interval *up* an octave as in (b).

How to Calculate Inversions

To calculate an inversion, subtract the interval from 9. For example, an inverted unison (1) is an octave (9 - 1 = 8). An inverted 2nd (2) is a seventh (9 - 2 = 7). An inverted sixth (6) results in a third (9 - 6 = 3), and so on.

When a perfect interval is inverted, the result is always another perfect interval.

Table 5-3

original intervals	*inverted intervals*
unison	octave
4th	5th
5th	4th
octave	unison

The inversion of *major* intervals always results in *minor* intervals and, conversely, the inversion of minor intervals results in major invervals.

Table 5-4

original	*inverted*
m2	M7
M2	m7
m3	M6
M3	m6
m6	M3
M6	m3
m7	M2
M7	m2

The inversion of diminished intervals produces augmented intervals and the inversion of augmented intervals produces diminished intervals.

Table 5-5

original	inverted
d4	A5
A4	d5
d5	A4
A5	d4
d8	A1

Summary

This table summarizes the inversion of intervals discussed so far.

Table 5-6

original	inverted
perfect	perfect
major	minor
minor	major
diminished	augmented
augmented	diminished

(1) Invert each interval given on the following staff by moving the bottom note up an octave. The bottom note of the inverted interval is given. Write the name of the original and inverted intervals in the spaces below the staff.

(a)   (b)   (c)   (d)

- - - - - - - - - - - - - -

(1)

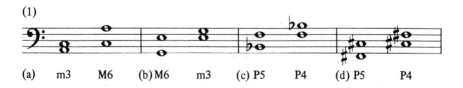

(a)   m3   M6   (b) M6   m3   (c) P5   P4   (d) P5   P4

(2) Invert each interval on the following staff by moving the top note down an octave. Write the names of the original and inverted intervals on the lines below them.

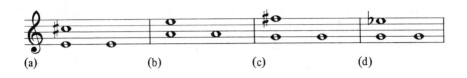

(a)   (b)   (c)   (d)

---

(2)

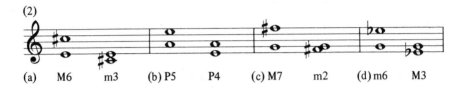

(a)   M6   m3   (b) P5   P4   (c) M7   m2   (d) m6   M3

How to Read Intervals

It's important to be able to recognize intervals on the staff quickly, because it's often much easier to read and write music by intervals rather than by working with the names of notes and their locations on a musical instrument. Let's look at some basic intervals with an eye toward the visual appearance of each interval on the staff. Doing this, you'll begin to see how interval recognition can help you improve your ability to deal with written notation. We've already shown you how to calculate intervals: here we give you some tips to help you recognize them quickly, as old friends. Let's start with one of the most easily recognized intervals, the second.

The second

Seconds

With seconds, if the lower note is on a line, the upper note will be on a space, and if the lower note is on a space, the upper note will be on a line. Also, to be a second, the upper note must be on the first available line or space.

Fifths

Another interval that is fairly easy to recognize is the fifth. Here are more examples of fifths.

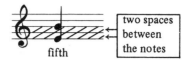

Notice that both notes are line notes. Also, notice that there are two spaces running between the notes.

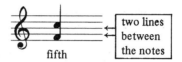

Notice that both notes are space notes. There are two lines between the notes.

As quickly as you can, label each of the following as "2" (for second) or "5" (for fifth) or "N" for neither second nor fifth. Write your answer on the spaces provided beneath the intervals.

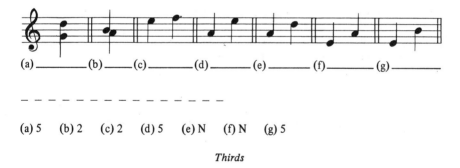

(a) 5   (b) 2   (c) 2   (d) 5   (e) N   (f) N   (g) 5

Thirds

The interval of a third looks somewhat similar to a fifth. Examine the illustrations below and answer these questions. The questions are designed to help you find out in what way a third is similar and in what way it is different from a fifth:

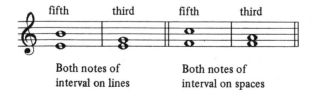

Both notes of   Both notes of
interval on lines   interval on spaces

(1) If the lower note of a fifth is a line-note, the upper note is always a line-note. Is this also true of thirds?   Yes ____ No ____

(2) If the lower note of a fifth is a space-note, the upper note will be a space note, too. Is this also true of thirds?   Yes ____ No ____

(3) A third looks different from a fifth in that the notes are: [closer together—further apart] (pick one).

(4) A third made up of space-notes always has [one—two line(s)] (pick one) in between the notes.

(5) A third made up of line-notes always has [one—two space(s)] (pick one) in between the notes.

– – – – – – – – – – – – – – – –

(1) Yes: a third is made up of either two line notes or two space notes.
(2) Yes: a third is made up of either two line notes or two space notes.
(3) A third looks different from a fifth in that the notes are closer together.
(4) A third made up of space-notes always has one line between the notes.
(5) A third made up of line-notes always has one space between the notes.

Identify the following intervals as either 2 (second), 3 (third), or 5 (fifth). Work quickly. Write the appropriate number in the box below each interval.

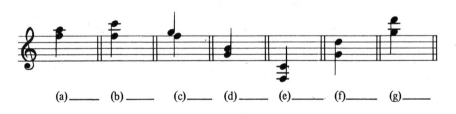

(a) ____   (b) ____   (c) ____   (d) ____   (e) ____   (f) ____   (g) ____

– – – – – – – – – – – – – – –

(a) 3   (b) 5   (c) 2   (d) 3   (e) 5   (f) 5   (g) 5

In the exercise above did you find item (g) more difficult than item (f)?   Yes ____ No ____

If you said "Yes": Perhaps you are not paying attention to the attributes that we mentioned earlier. Item (g) should be just as easy as item (f), since both intervals are composed of line-notes with two spaces in between. The fact that notes in item (g) are high up on the staff should not make any difference.

If you said "No": Excellent. Apparently you are able to focus on the critical attributes of the intervals and you aren't bothered by the placement of the intervals on or above the staff.

It is very helpful to use what you know about intervals when reading music. It is just as easy to read high notes (or low notes) as notes in the middle of the staff when you know how many lines and spaces there are in an interval. A fifth is a fifth no matter where it appears. This principle is so important that we're going to give you some more practice in applying it. This time, let's work with some low notes.

Suppose that you know that this note is C.

Even if you don't know the names of notes lower or higher than this, you can quickly read them by using your ability to recognize intervals. For example, suppose you come upon this note:

A difficult note? Hardly. All you need to do is visualize the note C (which you already know):

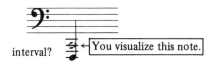

interval?   You visualize this note.

After visualizing the note C, you simply decide what the interval is between the real note and your visualized note. What is the interval? _____

– – – – – – – – – – – – – – –

A fifth. Now to get the letter name of that low note all you need do is count down a fifth from C to F (See pages 9 through 16 if you want to review names of lines and spaces).

Now that you have a better idea of how a knowledge of intervals can help you in reading music, let's look at the rest of the intervals up to the octave. In fact, let's look at examples of each of these intervals (even the ones we've already covered).

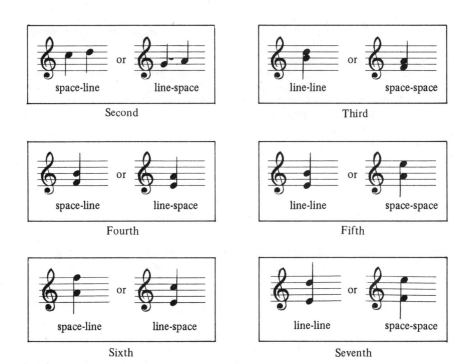

Study the intervals and look for some differences and commonalities among them. After making your own observations, read over the ones we've made:

All the odd-numbered intervals (third, fifth, seventh) have notes of the same kind: both space-notes or both line-notes.

The third, fifth, and seventh can be quickly distinguished from one another by the distance between the notes.

Third	Fifth	Seventh
Two line notes or two space notes rather close together	Two line notes or two space notes moderately close together	Two line notes or two space notes spread far apart

All of the even-numbered intervals have notes of opposite kinds: line–space or space–line. The second and octave are also line–space or space–line intervals.

The second is made up of notes that are hugging each other.

The octave always has three lines between its notes.

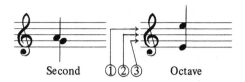

The rule that an octave always has three lines separating its notes can be quite helpful in reading or writing octaves. Which of these are octaves?

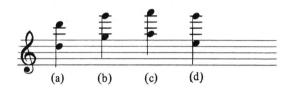

– – – – – – – – – – – – – – –

(a), (b), (c): (d) has four lines between the notes.

Once you're good at recognizing a fifth, it will be fairly easy for you to learn to spot fourths and sixths. Consider the appearance of a sixth. Notice how the upper note of a sixth may be visualized as one step above the upper note of a fifth.

Similarly, a fourth may be visualized as one step lower than a fifth.

(1) Give the interval name of each of these intervals (5 for fifth, etc).

(a)   (b)   (c)   (d)   (e)   (f)   (g)   (h)

- - - - - - - - - - - - - - -

(a) 5   (b) 2   (c) 3   (d) 5   (3) 6   (f) 8   (g) 7   (h) 4

(2) Write a note that is an octave below each of these notes.

- - - - - - - - - - - - - -

(2)

Aural Identification of Intervals

Being able to hear intervals is just as valuable as learning to identify them visually. This will come in handy if you want to

- Conduct a musical group
- Sing a melody or hear it in your imagination when you read music
- Write down music that you hear or compose yourself
- Hear the intervals a composer is using when you listen to a piece of music

Here you'll learn one way to hear intervals—by associating well-known melodies: example, the first two notes from a familiar theme popularly known as "Here Comes the Bride" form a perfect fourth. Eventually, with practice, you'll be able to recognize an interval without associating it with the familiar tune that contains it. Try singing the tune.

Here   comes   the   bride

Finally, sing the tones on the syllable "lu" without thinking of the words. When you feel comfortable doing that, practice singing each of the following intervals, using the "hearing aids" given.

INTERVAL NAME	NOTATION	(WELL-KNOWN MELODIES) HEARING AID (Note: if you're not familiar with these examples or don't like them, you may wish to adopt your own. Do this by playing the interval on an instrument, if you can, and then thinking of a line from a song that contains the interval.
MINOR SECOND (m2)		"O Little Town of Bethlehem" O lit - tle town of m2 m2
PERFECT FOURTH (P4)		Here comes the bride P4
MAJOR SIXTH (M6)		"My Bonnie Lies Over the Ocean" My bon - nie lies M6

(Note: We'll cover the other intervals later.)

After you've practiced the previous exercise so thoroughly that you feel you've mastered the sound of the m2, P4, and M6, check your mastery with these questions.

What interval is formed when the designated words of each of these songs is sung? Pick one answer.

(1) "My Country 'Tis of Thee . . ."

          ↱↑

   (a) m2
   (b) P4
   (c) M6

(2) "N-B-C" (TV network theme song)

      ↱↑

   (a) m2
   (b) P4
   (c) M6

(3) "Should Old Acquaintance . . ." ("Auld Lang Syne")

      ↱___↑

   (a) m2
   (b) P4
   (c) M6

(4) "Oh give me a home . . ." ("Home on the Range")

      ↱_↑

   (a) m2
   (b) P4
   (c) M6

– – – – – – – – – – – – – –

(1) (a)   (2) (c)   (3) (b)   (4) (b)

(1)

(2)*

*"NBC CHIMES" is a registered servicemark of the National Broadcasting Company, Inc. Reprinted with permission.

(3)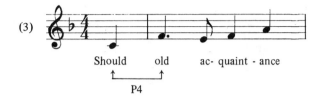

(4)

If you missed any of these, you may wish to play the intervals on a musical instrument and associate the interval names with the tunes given.

Hearing Aids

Now, using the complete table of intervals and hearing aids given below, practice singing each interval as before. (Review the minor second, major sixth, and perfect fourth if you feel you need to.)

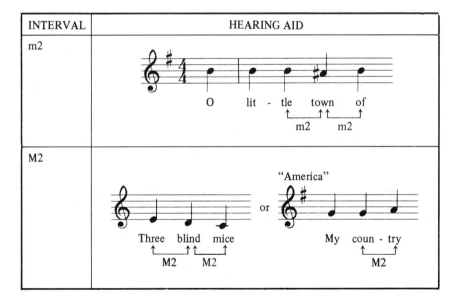

INTERVAL	HEARING AID
m2	O lit - tle town of — m2 m2
M2	Three blind mice — M2 M2 or "America" My coun - try — M2

INTERVAL	HEARING AID
m3	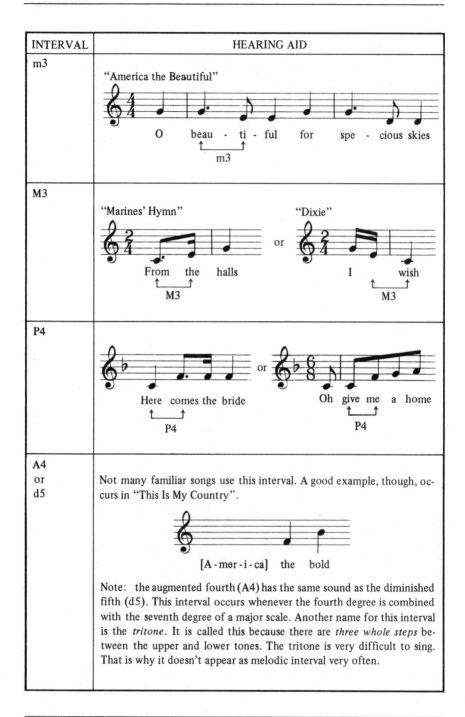
M3	
P4	
A4 or d5	Not many familiar songs use this interval. A good example, though, occurs in "This Is My Country". Note: the augmented fourth (A4) has the same sound as the diminished fifth (d5). This interval occurs whenever the fourth degree is combined with the seventh degree of a major scale. Another name for this interval is the *tritone*. It is called this because there are *three whole steps* between the upper and lower tones. The tritone is very difficult to sing. That is why it doesn't appear as melodic interval very often.

INTERVAL	HEARING AID
P5	"Erie Canal" — I got a mule her — P5 / "Feelings"* — Feel-ings — P5 / or — Kum-ba ya my Lord — ·P5 — First and third notes
M6	"My Bonnie Lies Over the Ocean" — My bon-nie lies — M6
A5 or m6	This interval doesn't occur often in well-known songs. Practice it by first singing a perfect fifth and then singing up a half step. Next sing the lower tone, imagine the interval of a fifth and then sing a half step up from the imagined note. Finally, sing the A5 (m6) directly without the intervening note. Suggestion: get a record of Chopin's Waltz in C♯-minor; the first two pitches form a m6.

*"Feelings"–English words and music by Morris Albert.
Reprinted with permission of Fermata International Melodies, Inc.

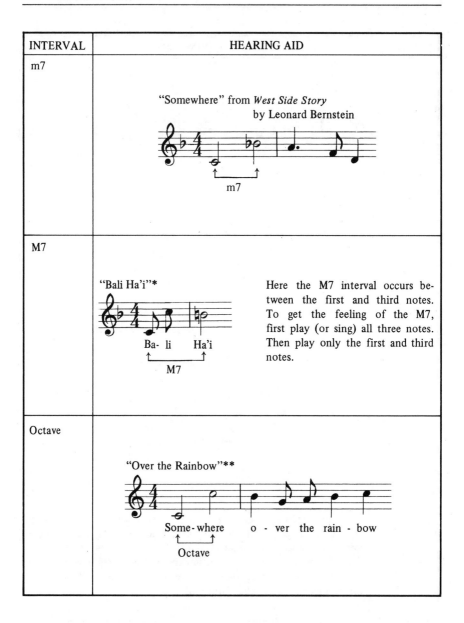

INTERVAL	HEARING AID
m7	"Somewhere" from *West Side Story* by Leonard Bernstein
M7	"Bali Ha'i"* — Here the M7 interval occurs between the first and third notes. To get the feeling of the M7, first play (or sing) all three notes. Then play only the first and third notes.
Octave	"Over the Rainbow"**

Now, test yourself. What interval is formed when the designated words of each of these songs is sung?

(1) "Row, row, row your boat. . ."
    └──↑

(2) "My coun-try 'tis of thee . . ."
    ↑──↑

(3) ". . . Sweet land of liberty . . ."
    ↑──↑

(4) ". . . of thee I sing."
    ↑──↑

(5) ". . . of thee I sing. Land where my . . ."
    ↑───↑

(6) "Oh say! Can you see . . ."
    ↑──↑

(7) ". . . by the dawn's ear-ly light . . ."
    ↑───↑

(8) "Mi-chelle, ma belle. These are words that go to-geth-er well . . ."
    (Skip the note on the syllable "to.")   ↑───↑

(9) "Hey Jude, don't make it bad, take a sad song . . ."
    (Skip the notes on "a sad.")   ↑─────↑

(10) "O my dar-ling O my dar-ling . . ." ("Clementine")
     ↑──↑

– – – – – – – – – – – – – – – –

(1) m2   (2) m3   (3) m2   (4) M2   (5) P5   (6) P4   (7) m6   (8) d5   (9) m7
(10) M6

(See musical notation of these songs on the next page.)

Optional exercise: play and sing these examples on a musical instrument.

Additional Practice

It takes a lot of practice to develop a good ear for intervals, so you will probably want to work on your own. (Don't be discouraged if you don't learn to recognize all of them overnight.) For additional practice, you may wish to keep a notebook of intervals. Set aside a separate page for each interval. When you hear a new song that you like, analyze its melodic intervals. Make a note of the intervals that catch your ear. Record them on the appropriate pages in your notebook. You might also practice with a friend. Take turns playing, singing, and naming different intervals. In addition, you may wish to buy a prerecorded audio tape designed to help you develop your ear for intervals. (See the Appendix for a list of recommended study material.)

Summary

Here are the important ideas to remember from this chapter.

- Intervals can be *melodic* or *harmonic*.
- Interval names have numerical and nonnumerical components.
- An interval is inverted when the lower note is moved up to a higher octave to become the upper note or when the upper note is moved down to become the lower note.
- An important inversion is the inversion of a fifth to a fourth. That's because a fifth is considered appropriate in certain musical contexts but a fourth may not be.
- Different intervals have distinctive appearances in musical notation; you can learn to recognize them by their overall appearance and by counting lines and spaces on the staff.
- It's possible to read notes by paying attention to intervals rather than thinking about the exact letter names. This approach is especially effective when you are reading notes on ledger lines.
- A good way to learn to recognize the sound of various intervals is to associate them with well-known melodies.

CHAPTER SIX

Tonality

Tonality refers to the organization of all the tones in a piece of music. (The term key is often used interchangeably with tonality.) How can tones be organized? For one thing, some can be given more importance than others. As we've seen, tonal music is organized around a principle tone called a *keynote* or *tonic*. Tones can also be organized by assigning them certain tendencies. In tonal music, the seventh degree has a strong tendency to move upward to the eighth degree (or keynote). In this chapter you will learn some of the details about the organization of tonal music. Specifically, when you finish this chapter, you'll be able to

- Describe the main characteristic of tonal music
- Identify the keynote in a piece of music and give reasons for your choice
- Do an experiment with a piano to show that "overtones" (or "harmonics") are produced whenever a natural tone sounds
- Explain why the fifth degree dominates all other degrees in its relationship to the tonic
- Identify melodic movement that gives a stable feeling and explain why this is so
- Choose the note likely to occur next when given a series of notes in tonal music
- Identify harmonic resolutions that help to establish a tonal center

Degree Names and Their Relationships

Tonal music uses the degrees of the scale to establish tonal relationships. (If you want to review degrees of the scale, see pages 109 through 110.) A melody written in a major or minor key will move from one tone to the next according to those relationships. Each tone in a minor and major key has a unique quality of stability or tension because of its relationship to the tonic. Here is the scale of C-major with each degree named and numbered.

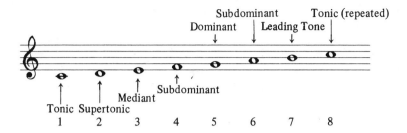

Now let's discuss each degree in detail. We'll start with the foundation of the scale, the tonic. Keep in mind that the name and characteristics for each degree apply to all the tones with the same letter names, in all other octaves.

The Tonic

As you've learned, the tonic (or keynote) is the tonal center around which all the other tones in the scale are organized. Many tonal songs begin with the tonic and nearly all end with the tonic. Also, the tonic is often accented. Notes of long duration, for example, frequently occur on the tonic. In addition, the tonic may be accented by being the highest or lowest note in a composition.

Here's an exercise you may wish to try on your favorite musical instrument to get a feeling for the magnetic quality of the tonic. Play these degrees of the C-major scale: 1-2-3-4-5-6-7-8. Now, do it again. Begin with the tonic and continue up the scale, but this time stop on the seventh degree (the leading tone). What feeling do you get?

— — — — — — — — — — — — — — —

You might have said: A movement of tones that stops one tone short of the tonic creates a feeling of tension. It seems like an uncompleted journey.

In a similar manner, a tonal movement that begins at the tonic and continues up or down an octave past the tonic to the next tone seems to have overshot the mark. Now let's see if you can apply this knowledge to a familiar song.

What is the tonic in "America"? How can you tell? (In what ways does it predominate?) (See notation on the next page.)

The tonic is _____ . I can tell because:

- - - - - - - - - - - - -

The tonic is F. The F appears twice at the beginning of the song in measure one, and also at the end, in measure fourteen. Also, the two longest notes in the song, the dotted whole notes in measures six and fourteen, are on F. The tonic is also emphasized by the frequent appearance of tones strongly related to it, as we shall soon see.

The Leading Tone (The Seventh Degree)

In major scales, a relationship that strongly emphasizes the tonic is the half-step interval that occurs between the seventh and eighth degrees (the eighth degree is really the same as the first degree; it's just an octave higher). Because the half step is the smallest interval in a scale, when it occurs between two tones it creates a strong sense of movement. The seventh degree leads up to the tonic. For this reason, the seventh degree is called the *leading tone*.

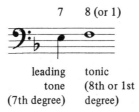

Let's look again at "America." Where in this song does the leading tone strengthen and give stability to the tonic?

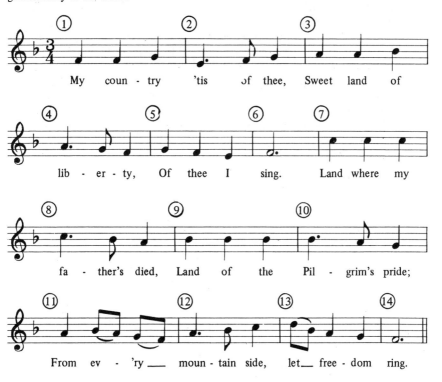

_ _ _ _ _ _ _ _ _ _ _ _ _ _ _

The tonic in measure six is strengthened and given additional stability by the leading-tone (E in measure five) that precedes it. Because the movement of leading tone to tonic has a feeling of conclusion, it is especially effective in drawing a melody or a section of melody to a close. In measure two, the leading tone also gives greater emphasis to the opening statements of the tonic.

The Leading Tone in Minor Keys

As you will recall, the natural minor scale has half steps between degrees two and three and degrees five and six, with whole steps everywhere else. (See page 93 for the natural minor scale.)

So the seventh degree in the natural minor isn't much of a leading tone. What can we do to change this seventh degree so it leads more strongly into the tonic?

_ _ _ _ _ _ _ _ _ _ _ _ _ _ _

Raise the seventh degree with an accidental.

The accidental that provides a leading tone in a minor scale melody can be a clue for identifying a minor key. If a melody with a three-flat signature (B♭, E♭, A♭) contained one or more B-naturals (B♮), it would be a strong indication that the melody is in C-minor, not E♭-major. To confirm this suspicion, one would look for C at the beginning and end of the melody; this emphasis would confirm that C is the tonic of the piece.

"Gentle Fair Jenny," a Kentucky mountain song, has a one-flat key signature that indicates either F-major or D-minor (relative minor) tonality. Examine the melody carefully and see if you can decide whether the key is F-major or D-minor.

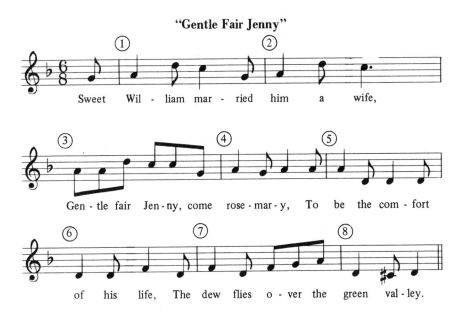

The C# accidental in the last measure is a dead giveaway for D-minor: the C# leads into D and is also preceded by D. In addition, D is the prominent note from measure five to the end. The D-minor tonality first suggested by the accidental is confirmed by this final emphasis on D.

For another example of this, let's look at the English ballad "Greensleeves." It has a one-sharp key signature that can indicate either the key of G-major or E-minor. What do you say? Is it in G-major or E-minor?

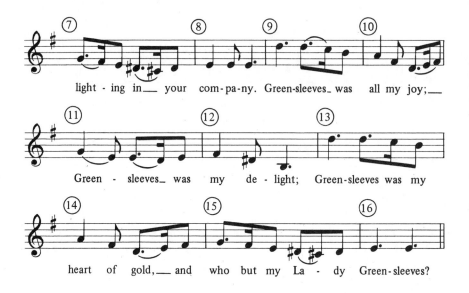

light - ing in__ your com-pa-ny. Green-sleeves_ was all my joy;__

Green - sleeves_ was my de - light; Green-sleeves was my

heart of gold,__ and who but my La - dy Green-sleeves?

The D♯ accidentals at measure four, seven, twelve, and fifteen support E-minor as a candidate for the key, especially since D♯ leads directly into E at the end of measures seven and fifteen. Here's more supporting evidence: Although neither the pitch E nor G is especially prominent at the beginning, E decidedly closes the song. Another bit of evidence is the raising of C to C♯ at measures seven and fifteen; this, as you may remember from Chapter Four, follows the harmonic minor scale pattern, which raises the sixth degree as well as the seventh in the ascending form.

So far we've discussed the tonic and its close friend, the leading tone. Another degree that has a strong relationship with the tonic is the fifth degree.

The Dominant (Fifth Degree)

The fifth degree is called the *dominant*. The strength of the relationship between the tonic and dominant lies in the importance of the fifth degree and the interval of a perfect fifth. The perfect fifth is an especially important interval.

Here's an experiment that will help you understand why. It requires a piano. If you don't have one, just read through it now. You may wish to try the experiment the next time you visit a music store.

1. Push down the damper pedal on a piano with your foot. This is usually the pedal furthermost to the right. (The damper pedal releases the felt pads that dampen the strings. With the damper pedal down, the strings are free to vibrate.)

2. Very gently push down the key for this note so it does *not* sound.

g

3. Strike this key sharply and then release it.

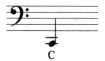

C

4. Take your foot off the damper pedal but keep holding down this key:

g

Describe what happened:

‒ ‒ ‒ ‒ ‒ ‒ ‒ ‒ ‒ ‒ ‒ ‒ ‒ ‒ ‒ ‒

If you did the experiment correctly, you should have heard the note g start to sound as if magically (since you never played it.) This happens because the tone g is contained within the tone C. When a string vibrates as a whole like this:

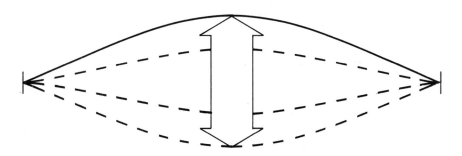

. . . it also vibrates as two half-lengths:

... and at the same time it vibrates as three third lengths:

Likewise, the same string vibrates in fourths and increasingly smaller segments. Each different vibrating length produces its own pitch. This means that one vibrating string actually produces several different pitches at the same time! Each separate pitch produced by the same vibrating string is called a *partial* or *harmonic*. All of the pitches produced by a single vibrating string are called a *harmonic series.*

The Harmonic Series

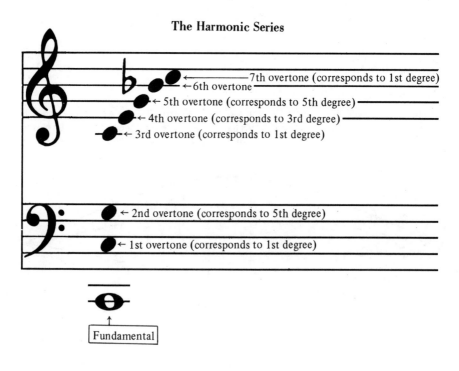

In the harmonic series the *fundamental* (in this case C) gives a tone its basic quality. Harmonics that are higher in pitch than the fundamental are called *overtones*. Of the overtones, the first (an octave higher than the fundamental) and the second (an octave and a *fifth* higher—the g) have the greatest intensity. They are, in general, easier to hear than the higher overtones.

It's important to note that the fifth degree of a scale is the same tone as the tonic's second overtone. So the fifth degree already participates in the sound of the tonic in a significant way. For this reason it *dominates* all the other scale degrees in the strength of its relationship to the tonic, hence, in Western music, the term *dominant* for the fifth degree.

The strength of the tonic-dominant relationship is not affected by the relative positions of the two tones: the dominant can be below or above the tonic. Above the tonic it sounds the interval of a perfect fifth. Below the tonic the interval is inverted to a perfect fourth.

Now let's look again at "America" to see how the dominant can effect the character of a melody. Start by examining just the first eight measures.

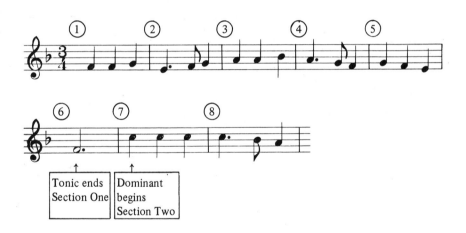

Note that the dominant (C) is absent for the first six measures. Measure six slows down the rhythm and ends on the tonic. The stability of the tonic here marks the melody's first resting point and rounds off the first section of the song. The appearance of the dominant in measure seven is striking for several reasons: the dominant (C) begins a new section. Its appearance here is especially strong because of the leap upward from tone one to tone five. Whenever you leap to a note by the interval of a fourth (or larger) you really stress the note that you are leaping to. Up to this point, the melody proceeds smoothly by steps, and after the introduction of the dominant in measure seven it continues in the same smooth stepwise motion. The first appearance of the dominant gives the song balance by introducing a fresh tonal character. (We also connect the dominant in the second section to the tonic at the beginning of the song because the rhythm of measures one and two is duplicated in the new section.)

The dominant also serves as a tonal focus for measures seven through eight:

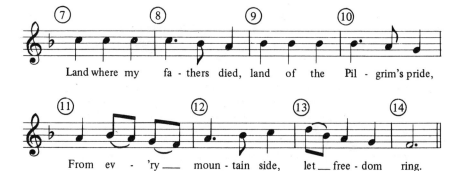

The melody here is within a 5–1–5–1 framework: slowly moving down from five, briefly touching on one (measure eleven) and then rebounding to five before the final two measures.

Many songs, especially folk songs, begin on the dominant and leap up to the tonic. This 5–1 melodic motion at the beginning firmly establishes the tonality of a piece. This technique gives folk songs a typically solid, stable feeling. The opening measures of "Home on the Range" shows the dominant–tonic opening:

Which of these songs starts with a melodic motion that strongly emphasizes the tonic?

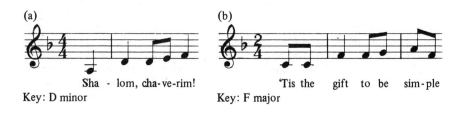

－ － － － － － － － － － － － －

Both songs are equally strong, as they start with 5-1 melodic movement. Though they both have the same key signature (a), d´is the tonic and in (b), f´is the tonic.

The Mediant (Third Degree)

The third degree occupies the midpoint between the tonic and the dominant.

Consequently it is called the *mediant*. The mediant of the major scale corresponds with the fourth overtone in the tonic's harmonic series, as we mentioned on page 144. (The lowered mediant of the minor scale does not correspond, but our ear attributes similar qualities to both.) The tonic, dominant, and mediant are the three stable tones of the major and minor scales. In fact when these three tones are sounded simultaneously they make a very stable sound, a sound that almost always occurs at the end of a tonal composition. (We cover triads in chapter 8.) This is because the keynote, when sounded alone, already contains the mediant and dominant as strong overtones.

The opening of the "Star-Spangled Banner" sounds especially stable and solid because of the way the melody leaps back and forth among the first, third, and fifth degrees:

The emphasis on these stable tones also contributes to the simplicity of children's songs like "Mary Had a Little Lamb" and "Three Blind Mice," shown here with degrees labeled.

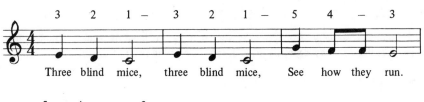

How Scale Degrees Affect Melody

A lot of melodies jump back and forth among the tonic, mediant, and dominant tones. In fact, one guideline for tonal melody writing that says that any movement among the tonic, mediant, and dominant degrees is generally a stable and pleasing melodic movement.

Examples (all in C-major):

Which of these melodies has a more stable feeling? Why?

— — — — — — — — — — — — — — —

Melody (a) is more stable because it skips among the tonic, mediant, and dominant degrees.

The Subdominant (Fourth Degree)

The fourth degree lies under the dominant and is called the *subdominant* (*sub* means under).

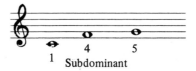

The stability of the subdominant is somewhat undermined by its nearness to the dominant; it tends to move up to the fifth degree as the dominant exercises its magnetizing power over the tones next to it.

Sometimes the subdominant is drawn down to the mediant. This is especially true in the major scale where the mediant is only a half step below the subdominant. This half step seems to exert another magnetizing force. This happens most often when the melody leaps up to the subdominant since after an upward leap there is a tendency for a melody to move downward by step. This is a natural melodic movement because a singer, having expelled a lot of energy to leap upwards, tends to want to relax by moving downwards by step.

Name the subdominants of these keys:

(a) G-major
(b) B♭-major
(c) F-minor
(d) C-minor
(e) E♭-major

— — — — — — — — — — — — — — —

(a) G-major: C
(b) B♭-major: E♭
(c) F-minor: B♭
(d) C-minor: F
(e) E♭-major: A♭

Using what you know about the tendency of the scale degrees to move in certain ways, see if you can tell what the next note would probably be in each of these incomplete examples. Several answers are acceptable, but take a guess. What note would be *most likely*, assuming that the last note follows its natural tendency. (Write that note on the staff.

(1)

Hint: Note how the tonic leaps up to the subdominant.

(2)

Hint: Here the subdominant is approached by step and the previous upward stepwise motion has established a pattern.

(3)

Assume that this is a melody to be sung and that the next note is a leap *up* from b′. What note is most likely if the music continues to focus on *stable* degrees?

(1)

In this example since we have skipped up to subdominant (C), it would be natural to fall back to the mediant (B). Other choices are also possible.

(2)

This time the subdominant is drawn up to the dominant (D). The scale passage helps to propel it upward.

(3)

Since the next note would be a leap *up* to a stable degree, the only other possible choices are g″ and b″. It would be difficult to sing a leap from b′ to g″ (a minor sixth). The note b″ is simply too high when you consider that the melody started with d′.

The Submediant (the Sixth Degree)

The sixth degree is the *submediant*. Its name comes from the fact that it lies a third *below* the tonic: the mediant, remember, is a third above the tonic.

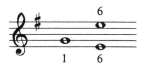

Being a neighbor to the dominant, the submediant easily falls within its sphere of influence; that is, the submediant is often drawn down to the dominant. This is especially true of the sixth degree of the minor scale which is strongly drawn to the dominant by virtue of the half step between the fifth and sixth degrees. As shown here, the sixth degree, E♭, leads naturally to the D, the dominant.

Key: G minor

Exercise

● Sing (or play on an instrument) an ascending major scale from 1 to 6, then back to 5: 1-2-3-4-5-6-5.
● Sing (or play on an instrument) an ascending *melodic minor* scale from 1 to 6, then back to 5: 1-2-3-4-5-6-5. Note how the submediant likes to move downward to the dominant.

(1) The sixth degree or _____ is unstable and tends to_____

(2) What would be the most obvious next note in this example:

Key: C major

- - - - - - - - - - - - - - - -

(1) Submediant; fall downward to the fifth degree or dominant

(2)

After leaping upward to the submediant, the melody tends to step down to the dominant.

The Supertonic (the Second Degree)

The second degree lies above the tonic and is called the *supertonic* (*super* means above). It is an active tone and tends to move down to the tonic or up to the mediant, as shown here:

Composers often use the supertonic and the leading tone to circle around the tonic (as in the first two measures of "America." "Circling around" means approaching the tone in

stepwise motion, from above and below. Any movement that circles around a particular tone emphasizes that tone. Here the supertonic emphasizes the tonic:

(1) Name the supertonic in these keys:
Db-major _____ G-minor_____ F-minor _____
B-major_____ C#-major _____ Bb-major _____

(2) The supertonic and leading tone are used to circle around the tonic in this example. In which measures does it occur? What is the effect of this circling?

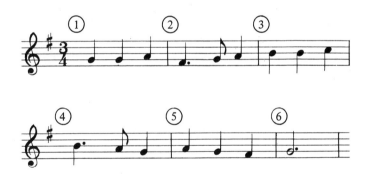

- - - - - - - - - - - - - - - -

(1) Db major: Eb   G-minor: A   F-minor: G
    B-major: C#   C#-major: D#   Eb-major: C

(2) Circling, which happens in measures one and two and measures five and six, strengthens or emphasizes the tonic g!

Summary of Scale Degree Names

This diagram summarizes the stable and active qualities of each of the scale degrees.

Notice that the stable degrees one, three, and five are located solidly on ground level and on plateaus at different heights. The active degrees stand unsteadily on a curved area and seem ready to move to a stable tone above or below it.

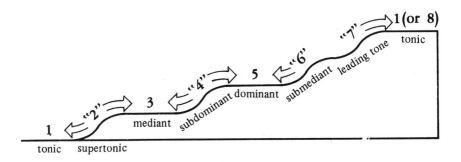

The Relative Stabiliy of the Scale Degrees

In each of the examples below put in the note you think would be the *most likely* note to come next. Base your answer on the material we've covered so far in this chapter. Make the note a half note.

Although other kinds of melodic movement are certainly possible, we think these are highly likely:

(1)

Submediant tends to move to dominant, especially when approached by skip from below.

(2)

Leading tone leads to tonic.

(3)

Supertonic tends to move to tonic or mediant.

(4)

Subdominant is drawn to dominant by upward scalewise motion.

(5)

Here the subdominant is approached by skip and tends to resolve downward to the mediant. Also, notice that a pattern has been established: up a third, down a second; up a third, down a second.

*These numbers show scale degrees.

Consonance, Dissonance, and Tonality

Each harmonic interval has a characteristic quality of rest and stability or instability and tension. The dynamic quality produced by sounds having tension or instability gives a feeling of tonal movement. A feeling of flow comes about as a result of alternating intervals of tension with intervals of rest. In music, the quality of rest and stability is called *consonance*, and the quality of tension or instability is called *dissonance*.

Consonance and dissonance are not easy to pin down. Consonance and dissonance have been heard differently by different cultures, historical periods, or even different individuals. The following table shows the changes in the sound of consonance and dissonance in Western music.

Table 6-1

Historical changes in the Western perception of consonance and dissonance.

Historical Framework	Considered a CONSONANCE	Considered a DISSONANCE
Middle Ages (modality)	8ve P4 P5	M3 m3 M6 m6 M2 m2 M7 m7 A4(d5)
1700–1900 (tonality)	8ve P4 P5 M3 m3 M6 m6	M2 m2 M7 m7 A4(d5)

*The perfect fourth is considered a consonance when it is used simultaneously with a third. When used alone, however, it is considered dissonant.

Another way of emphasizing the relative nature of consonance and dissonance is to consider two imaginary pieces of music with a different interval content. (Assume the first composition consists entirely of octaves and fifths and the second composition consists of major seconds and major sevenths.) In the first piece, a major third would sound dissonant. In the second, a major third would sound consonant. In our discussion of consonance and dissonance, we use the framework of the second historical period (1700 to 1900) because its harmonic style characterizes a larger part of the concert and popular music repertoire of today.

Not all consonant intervals are equally consonant, nor dissonant intervals equally dissonant. In the illustration below we show a progression from consonance to dissonance.

Greater Consonance ⟵————————————⟶ Greater Dissonance

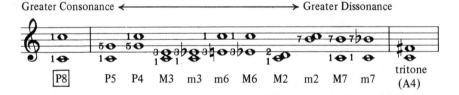

| P8 | P5 | P4 | M3 | m3 | m6 | M6 | M2 | m2 | M7 | m7 | tritone (A4) |

Note that the octave on the far left represents complete stability or consonance: both tones have equal strength. On the opposite end of the consonant-dissonant continuum is the tritone which represents complete dissonance because each tone sets up an overtone series that conflicts with the other.

Resolution: The Movement from Dissonance to Consonance

Movement from dissonance to consonance is another factor that helps to create a key feeling, or tonality. The movement from a dissonant interval to a consonant interval is called a *resolution*. A dissonance is resolved by a movement to a consonance.

Dissonance   Resolution   Consonance

A strong dissonance occurs whenever the fourth degree sounds with the seventh degree. This is tricky because at first glance the interval looks like a perfect fourth:

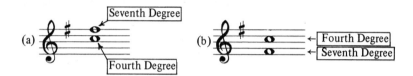

Actually, though, if you look closely, you'll see that Example (a) is an augmented fourth and Example (b) is a diminished fifth. (See Chapter 5 if you'd like to review this.)

In each example below circle the dissonance and the resolution of that dissonance. Label the dissonance D and the resolution R.

- - - - - - - - - - - - - - - - - -

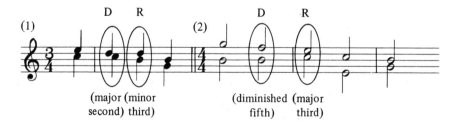

(1) What are the characteristics of
    (a) A dissonant interval?
    (b) A consonant interval?

(2) The movement from a dissonant to a consonant interval is called:

(3) Harmonic movement is created by what kinds of patterns?

(4) Do you think dissonant tension is *always* immediately resolved to consonant stability?

- - - - - - - - - - - - - - - -

(1) (a) Tension, instability, the tendency to move
    (b) Stability, rest, a starting point or a goal of tonal movement
(2) Resolution
(3) Patterns of consonance and dissonance
(4) No. Harmonic movement results from increasing dissonant tension as well as from resolving it.

As we mentioned earlier, the resolution of a dissonance can help to establish a tonal center. This happens when one of the tones of the dissonant interval is the leading tone and the other is the subdominant. Here's an example:

tritone minor sixth

Notice that the leading tone follows its natural tendency and moves upward to the *tonic*. The subdominant follows its tendency to move downward to the mediant. Notice too that both the leading tone and subdominant are active tones, whereas the tonic and mediant are stable tones.

Here are two examples of dissonance-consonance movement. Which establishes a tonal center more strongly?

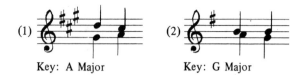

(1) Key: A Major   (2) Key: G Major

The key of A is established in (1), where the tritone interval (diminished fifth) resolves to a major third. The key is established because the leading tone moves up to the tonic and the subdominant moves down to the mediant. In (2) there is no leading tone. Also notice that in (2) the upper note is the mediant in both intervals. Since the mediant is a stable degree, there is no feeling of movement from instability to stability. Although both resolutions emphasize a tonal center, the first is stronger since it involves movement of both tones, one of which is the *leading* tone.

Summary

We've covered a lot of points in this chapter. Let's review the most important ones.

- Tonality refers to the organization of tones in a piece of music around a keynote (or tonic).
- Each degree of the scale has its own unique quality of stability or tension because of its relationship to the tonic.
- The first, third, and fifth degrees have a stable quality.
- The second, fourth, sixth, and seventh degrees are active; they have a tendency to move toward nearby stable degrees.
- A movement from dissonance to consonance can be used to strengthen a tonal center. This occurs, for example, when the leading tone forms an harmonic interval of a tritone with the subdominant. The leading tone resolves upward to the keynote, while the subdominant resolves downward to the mediant.

CHAPTER SEVEN

Musical Form and Design

Music becomes more meaningful for us when we begin to hear connections, when we hear the large-dimension forms made by the overall flow of tones. Composers group and organize musical fragments into larger, more meaningful units. In this chapter, we consider the overall shape of a melody as well as the smaller units from which it is constructed. When you finish this chapter, you will be able to

- Recognize desirable melodic contours
- Identify the *culmination point* in a melody
- Tell what the *range* of a melody is
- Identify these melodic units when given the notation for a melody:
  Motive
  Phrase
  Part
  Song form (two- and three-part)
- Compose (yes, compose!) melodic phrases by varying a given motive in specific ways
- Recognize the reappearance of a motive in varied form
- Analyze a melody and explain its form (You'll be able to say things like, "This melody is a tripartite song form.")

Melody has two basic components: melodic contour and rhythm. Both components work together to give a melody its distinctiveness. We'll discuss each of these components separately, starting with melodic contour.

Melodic Contour

If you were to draw a line connecting the notes of a melody, you would draw the contour of that melody. The rise and fall of the melodic line reveals the overall pattern of pitch movement. Melodic contour also shows the range of a melody, that is, its highest and lowest points.

(1) Draw a line connecting up these notes to reveal the contour of the melody:

America

(2) Focus on the contour line. Which of these does it look like the most?
   (a) city skyline
   (b) a bumpy road
   (c) a mountain range

- - - - - - - - - - - - - - - -

(1)

(2) (c)

"Mountain Range" Contour

The contour of most tonal melodies is often like that of a gentle mountain range, that is, the melodic line doesn't jump around aimlessly. Many tonal melodies start from a given low point and move upward to a *single* high point like a mountain peak. Frequently the melodic line then descends gradually to a low point somewhat near where it started. In moving upward, the line may occasionally fall back (just as a mountain range contour does), but the overall movement still progresses to a single high note called a culmination point.

Which of these would make a good traditional melodic line, one that fits the description we just gave?

(1)

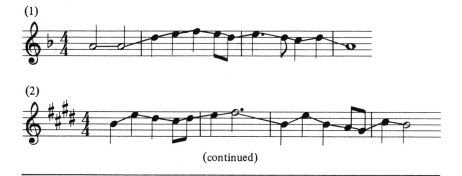

(2)

(continued)

(3)

(4)

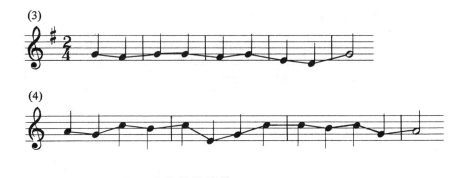

– – – – – – – – – – – – – – – –

The melodic lines (1) and (2) have good contours. Melody (1) is an excerpt from "Yesterday" by John Lennon and Paul McCartney.

Melody (2) is from Tchaikovsky's Trio in A-minor, Opus 50 (last movement).

Notice how both (1) and (2) start on a relatively low note, move up to a high culmination point (like a mountain peak), and then gradually return to the note from which they started. In (3), the melody doesn't go anyplace; it just hovers around g'. Example (4) has more shape than (3), but notice that the high note (c") is repeated five times; consequently, there is no culmination point. Melody (3) has the same weakness.

The examples we've just looked at are really just small fragments from longer pieces of music. It's important to realize that this "mountain range" type of contour may also be seen in larger sections of music, even in extended musical compositons.

Many tonal melodies have this type of structure. Some may start low and progress to a culmination point and end on it. This produces a dramatic ending because (1) it is a somewhat unusual pattern and (2) because high notes are naturally dramatic. (It takes more energy to sing them, and they tend to be performed more loudly than lower notes). Other melodies may start with relatively high notes, gradually drop down to lower notes and then climb up again to a culmination point. Various patterns are possible. The point is that most melodies have a definite shape; they go somewhere, rather than just weaving around a single note or two. Now that you're familiar with this "mountain range" quality, we'll consider some other characteristics of melodic lines.

Pitch Range

A related characteristic of melody is called "pitch range," which simply refers to the *interval* between the highest and lowest notes. Let's compare these two familiar melodies. First, connect up the notes to make the contours stand out. Then answer the following questions:

(a)

Oh___ say can you see by the dawn's ear - ly light,

(b)

My coun - try 'tis of thee, Sweet land of lib - er - ty

(1) Which example has the greater range?
(2) What is the interval range of example (a)?
(3) Of (b)?
(4) Which have a "mountain range" quality?

— — — — — — — — — — — — — — —

(1) (a)
(2) A tenth (from b to d″)
(3) A fifth (from f♯′ to c″)
(4) Both

Most simple folk tunes have a range of about an octave. The smallest range is of about a sixth. Children's songs, on the other hand, are often limited to a fifth.

Melodies with a range greater than an octave usually have a more dynamic quality, perhaps because of the increased energy required to reach up to the higher notes. Part of the dramatic effect of "The Star-Spangled Banner" is due to its extremely wide range—a twelfth!

Think for a moment about some of the Beatles' songs that you may have heard. What do you think is the typical range for their melodies?
—a fifth or less
—a fifth to an octave
—greater than an octave

— — — — — — — — — — — — — — —

Most have a range greater than an octave, the most common range being that of a tenth or eleventh.

Conjunct and Disjunct Motion

Another feature of a melody is the nature of the movement from note to note. Movement among notes can be classified as *conjunct* or *disjunct*. Conjunct movement (also called *stepwise* motion) is really another word for melodic notes that are a whole step or half step apart. The following notes show conjunct motion:

Conjunct (stepwise) motion

(*Conjunct* comes from the root word *con* meaning together and *junct* meaning joined.) Disjunct movement is movement by any interval greater than a whole step. Disjunct movement is also called "leaping." Here's an example:

Disjunct (leaping) motion

(The root word *dis* means apart, so literally, *disjunct* means joined apart.)

Let's look again at a few bars from "America" and "The Star-Spangled Banner." How do they compare with respect to conjunct and disjunct movement?

Star-Spangled Banner

America

(1) Is either example made up of entirely disjunct or conjunct motion?
(2) What kind of movement characterizes each example?
    "The Star-Spangled Banner":   conjunct   disjunct
    "America":   conjunct   disjunct

— — — — — — — — — — — — — — —

(1) No. Neither example uses exclusively disjunct or conjunct motion.
(2) "The Star-Spangled Banner" uses mainly disjunct motion; "America," conjunct motion.

Most melodies have a balance between conjunct and disjunct motion. Too much conjunct movement tends to put listeners to sleep; it's not distinctive enough to be interesting. Too much disjunct movement tends to make the melody sound too jerky or *disjointed*. In "The Star-Spangled Banner" excerpt, there are seven disjunct movements (melodic leaps). But this is balanced by three stepwise (conjunct) movements. Notice, too, that the disjunct movement takes place among the stable degrees of the scale: the tonic, mediant and dominant.

Here are three melodies. If possible, try them out with an instrument. Which one do you like best? Which one follows the guideline about balancing conjunct and disjunct movement?

(1)

(2)

(3)

— — — — — — — — — — — — — —

Melody (3) has the best balance. Melody (1) uses *all* disjunct movement. (It's difficult to sing because of this and lacks balance.) Melody (2) uses only conjunct movement. It sounds smooth and it's easy to sing, but it's also easy to forget because it lacks character. In (3) we see a good balance of leaps and steps: four disjunct movements and four conjunct. Melody (3) is from Mendelssohn's "Songs Without Words," No. 1.

So far we've looked at these aspects of melodic contour:

● "Mountain range" quality (up and down movement progressing to a culmination point and then descending gradually)

- Pitch range (interval between highest and lowest note)
- Conjunct and disjunct motion

Now let's consider the rhythmic aspect of melody.

To rephrase what we've said so far, melody is a series of tones of specific rhythm, moving up and down, organized into a unique, recognizable whole. We stress the word rhythm because melody, by its nature, cannot be separated from rhythm. When we respond to melody, we respond to pitch changes, but we also respond to rhythmic movement.

Name That Tune

You can demonstrate to yourself that rhythm is an important component of melody by trying this experiment. Think of a song that both you and a friend know. If possible, play (or hum) the melody on an instrument, but change the rhythm. If the melody is "On Top of Old Smoky," for example, instead of playing it like this:

... you might play it like this:

See if your friend can recognize the melody. Chances are he or she may find it difficult. If you can, try out our variation of the "Old Smoky" melody. Notice how different it sounds even though it uses exactly the same notes in exactly the same sequence.

Here's a related experiment: Think of a familiar melody. Then tap or clap just the rhythm of that melody. See if your friend can guess the name of that tune. Then reverse roles and see if you can name the tune when your friend taps out the rhythm. You may be surprised at how often you can guess correctly on the basis of just the rhythm.

Composers often use the power of rhythm to give variety to their music or conversely, to provide unity. To use rhythm to give *variety*, they may deliberately change the rhythm of the melody while keeping same scale degrees. In the next example, notice how the notes g', c ", d ", and e " are repeated with a different rhythm.

To provide *unity*, they may repeat a certain distinctive rhythm while changing the scale degrees. In the following example, the same rhythm in (a) is repeated in (b) with a different sequence of notes.

(a)   (b)

Here are some more examples. Look them over carefully with these questions in mind:

(1) In which example is rhythm used to provide variety? Explain how this is done.
(2) In which example is rhythm used to provide unity? Explain.
(3) What can you say about the rhythmical *accents* in the example that illustrates variety through rhythmic change? Are the same tones accented in the two versions of the melody?

Example (a)

"Joe Magarac" by Jacob A. Evanson, in *In Our Country* By James L. Mursell and others.
Publisher: California State Department of Education, 1958.

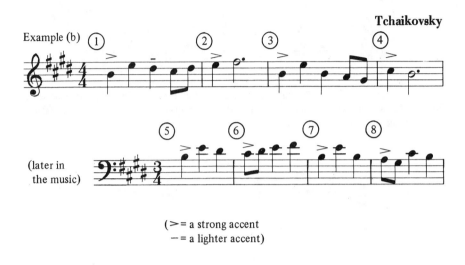

(> = a strong accent
  − = a lighter accent)

_ _ _ _ _ _ _ _ _ _ _ _ _ _ _

(1) Example (a) uses rhythm to provide unity. The rhythm ♩ ♫♩ ♩ appears in measure one and is repeated in measure five. Also, notice the rhythm in measures five and seven: ♩ ♩ ♫♩
It is very similar to the rhythm in measure one. The only difference is that the eighth notes (♫) now appear on beat three instead of beat two.

(2) Example (b) uses rhythm to provide variety. The letter names of the notes in measures one through four are the same as those in measures five through eight (with the rhythm changed). Some variety comes from the different octave in which the notes appear, but most of the variety is due to the rhythmic changes. Notice that the f♯″ in measure two is a dotted half note. In measure six when the corresponding f♯′ appears, it is a quarter note. Also, notice that different tones are accented in measures five through eight than in measures one through four. This is due to the shift from $\frac{4}{4}$ to $\frac{3}{4}$ meter.

Now that you have an understanding of some of the key aspects of melodic contour and rhythm, let's take a closer look at the ways composers often use these qualities to expand small melodic ideas into full-blown melodies.

Melodic Units

The smallest unit of a melody that can express an idea is called a *motive*. The next larger unit is called a *phrase*. Phrases may be organized into larger sections of music called *parts* or into specialized sections called *periods*. The parts (or periods), in turn, are often organized into an even larger section called a *song form*. Finally, in larger pieces of music, song forms are organized into *compound song forms*. We'll now discuss each of these units in detail beginning with the smallest—the motive.

The Motive

As we just mentioned, the *motive* is the smallest melodic unit that can express an idea. It is the basic building block, the "germ," which will change as the melody gradually reveals itself to the listener. It only takes two notes to make a motive if the notes are sufficiently distinctive, that is, easy to recognize because of their clear-cut characteristics. This motive, for example, appears in Beethoven's Piano Sonata, opus 2 no. 2.

These notes are distinctive because

- The first note begins on an upbeat. The eighth rest preceding a″ makes it clear the a″ occurs on the up part of the beat.
- There is a leap from the first to the second note. Any leap of a fourth or more is rather distinctive.

Motive Variations

We said that a motive changes as a melody unfolds. This is called motivic variation. Such variation helps to keep the melody interesting. The fact that the motive is still recognizable (even in its varied form) helps to unify the melody and make it understandable as a meaningful whole rather than a series of unrelated notes. There are a number of things a composer can do to create motivic variations, such as:

- Changing the order of the notes:

Original motive

Variation

- Adding intervening notes so that the disjunct motion is changed to conjunct motion:

- Changing the rhythm:

In this example notice that the first note (a″) now occurs on an accented beat and the second note (e″) on an unaccented beat.

- Using contrary motion, that is, keeping the intervals the same but making the notes move in the *opposite* direction. If the original notes go *up*, the notes in the variation go down and vice versa. Suppose the motive is:

Melodic intervals: 3   3   2   2   2   2   5

A contrary motion variation might be:

Melodic intervals: 3   3   2   2   2   2   5

- Keeping the melodic contour and rhythm the same, but using different scale degrees. (This kind of variation is called a "sequence.")

Original motive   Variation (sequence)

● Keeping the rhythm the same, but changing the melodic contour and scale degrees:

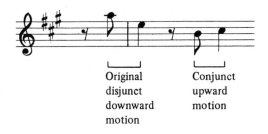

Original   Conjunct
disjunct   upward
downward   motion
motion

Exercise

(1) In this application, you get some guided practice in composing variations. All the variations will be based on this motive:

Key of C-major:

(We have numbered each note to simplify our directions.)

First, let's create a variation by changing the order of the notes.
Directions: Keep the rhythm the same, but change the order. Start with note 4 and go backwards from 3 to 2 to 1.

Many other such variations are possible by simply rearranging the order of the notes. Experiment, if you like, by creating some variations of your own. Play or sing them. Let your ear be your guide in picking out the ones that work best.

(2) Now, using the same motive, let's compose another variation by adding *intervening notes*. In between notes 1 and 2, add an intervening note so that the melody goes stepwise up the scale. Keep the rhythm the same.

Your answer may have been like this:

Intervening note

As before, we suggest you experiment with your own such variations.

This time, let's change the rhythm, but keep same scale degrees. Substitute this rhythm for the original rhythm:

Now for a contrary motion variation. In addition to using contrary motion, vary the motive by beginning on the dominant (g′) instead of the tonic (c′). (We've put in the first two notes for you:)

Finally, let's construct a sequence variation. Keep the contour and rhythm the same but start the motive on the supertonic (the second scale degree). (In keeping the contours the same, make sure the numerical value of the intervals used in the variation is the same as that used in the original motive.

There are many other techniques for varying the motive, but these are some of the most important ones. Let's move on to the next larger melodic unit: the phrase.

The Phrase

A *phrase* is a natural division of a melody similar to a sentence in speech. It is a melodic unit that a singer would tend to sing in one breath. Two or more motives can combine to form a phrase:

Or sometimes the same motive will be repeated (usually in modified form) to produce a phrase:

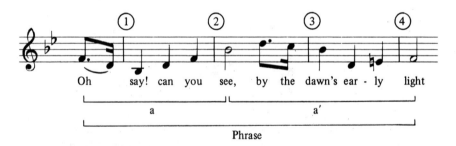

a = motive one
a' = first variation of motive one.

Look at the parts of the melody labeled *a* and *a'* in the excerpt from "The Star-Spangled Banner" given above. The part we call *a'* is really a repetition of the first motive in varied form. In what way is *a'* similar to *a*? (If you need a hint, peek below the first dotted line.)

— — — — — — — — — — — — — — —

Hint: Consider rhythm.

— — — — — — — — — — — — — — —

Both *a* and *a'* have exactly the same rhythm.
Here the rhythm gives the phrase unity while the different notes give it variety.

Now, you try it. Expand this motive into a phrase by using a sequence variation. Keep the rhythm and the numerical value of the intervals the same but use different scale degrees. Start the variation on the tonic.

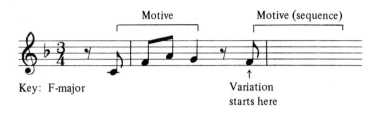

The Part

The _part_ as defined here is the next larger melodic unit after the phrase. A part is made up of any series of phrases that follow each other in close succession. The last phrase of the part is marked by a definite pause, called a cadence. (the word _cadence_ comes from the Latin word _cadere_ meaning to fall.) Instead of running on, the music "falls," that is, pauses or comes to a stop.) Although the cadence at the end of the first part is a definite one, it is not so definite that it dispels the expectation that another kindred part will follow.

Now let's put together some of the things you have learned and go through some of the thought processes a composer might use in composing a part.

In composing a melody, a good place to start is with the three stable degrees of the scale, which help establish the key (or tonality). What are they?

The tonic, mediant, and dominant (degrees one, three, and five).

Let's begin our melody with those stable degrees set to this rhythm:

Our melodic contour will be:

Ready? Write out the appropriate notes on the following staff in the key of C-major. (We've put in the first note for you.)

- - - - - - - - - - - - - - -

So far we've composed the first part of our motive. We've used a lot of disjunct motion. What might we do to balance that?

- - - - - - - - - - - - - - -

Use some conjunct motion.

We used stable degrees to get our melody off to a solid start. Let's balance that by moving up to the supertonic and then circling around it with conjunct motion:

We'll use these degrees and rhythm:

Finish the motive by putting in the notes as we've described them starting at the arrow.

Motive

Notice how these notes are circling around the supertonic.

Now that we have a motive, let's create a phrase.

On the staff below, extend this motive to a phrase by simply repeating the first six notes and then, in measure four, landing on the supertonic and staying there with a dotted quarter note.

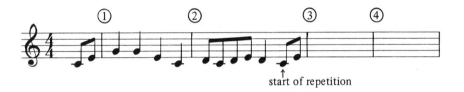

↑
start of repetition

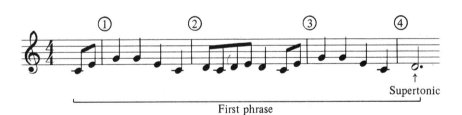

↑
Supertonic

First phrase

Notice that by ending the first phrase on the supertonic we have created a certain amount of tension since the supertonic is an active tone.

We can resolve this tension by composing a second phrase that brings us back to the tonic. Let us create the first six notes of this second phrase by using our old friend, the sequence variation. Here is the first note of the second phrase. You add five notes. (Notice that we now are starting the second phrase on the dominant , ᵍ .

End of first phrase

Second phrase

Now, instead of carrying on the sequence we'll change it slightly to emphasize the tonic with a 5–1 leap (remember, a leap from dominant to tonic).

Sequence broken to
return to tonic

Second phrase

Finally, we'll finish the second phrase. We'll do this by repeating the first four notes that the second phrase began with:

Second phrase

Then instead of repeating the next two notes of the second phrase (measures four and five), which are:

... we'll create a variation by adding the intervening notes c′ and a′:

Second phrase

Now we're ready to leap up to the final note of this part. What note do we leap up to? Write that note as a dotted half note on this staff:

- - - - - - - - - - - - - - -

By leading up to the tonic, we release the tension that was created by landing on the supertonic at the end of the first phrase.

Here's the complete melody, which makes up an entire part, or series of phrases.

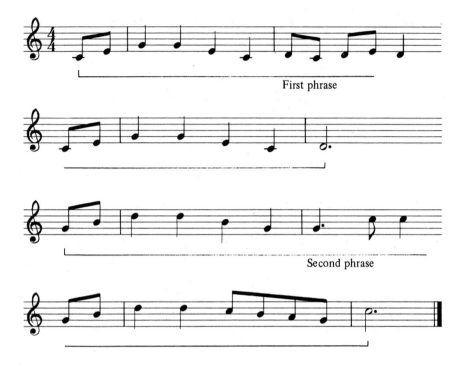

First phrase

Second phrase

Note: This part is actually an old folk song complete within itself.

Source: Percy Goetschins, *The Homophonic Forms of Musical Composition* (New York: Schirmer, 1898), p. 66.

Although a part may stand alone as a short musical composition, it may also be combined with other parts. (To review *part*, see page 175).

The Song Form

The *song form* results from combining two or more parts. (It's called a song form because originally it was used extensively with vocal pieces.) The parts are kindred (somewhat similar), yet they are different enough to stand alone as independent musical entities.

The Two-Part Song Form

In a two-part song form, the first part usually ends with a strong cadence on some degree other than the tonic. This way the listener expects more to come and feels a sense of conclusion when the last part ends with the tonic.

Now that you've been introduced to the motive, phrase, part, and song form, let's examine a piece known as the "Sicilian Hymn" and identify these various units. We've labeled some motives and their variations, but have left others blank.

a = Motive a   "a" = variation of Motive a.
b = Motive b   "b" = variation of Motive b.

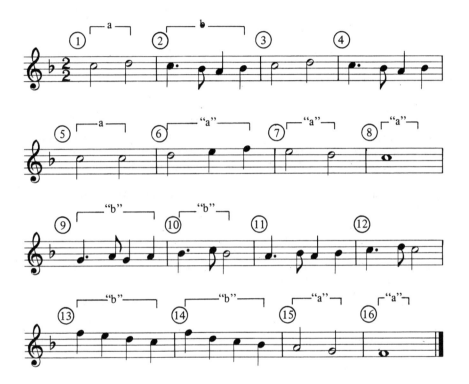

We'll begin by looking at the overall organization of this piece.

(1) What measures make up part one?
(2) What measures make up part two?
(3) Which measures make up what we might call the two-part song form?
(4) In which measures are there strong cadences?
(5) (a) Does part one cadence on the tonic?
    (b) Does part two cadence on the tonic?

— — — — — — — — — — — — — — —

(1) Measures one through eight
(2) Measures nine through sixteen
(3) Measures one through sixteen.
(4) The strong cadence in measure eight marks the end of part one; a similar cadence in measure sixteen marks the end of part two
(5) (a) No. This is typical. Usually part one cadences on some tone other than the tonic, such as the dominant.
  (b) Yes

Now let's look at the motives.

This hymn opens with two slow-moving notes: (♩ ♩) This is motive *a*. In the next measure, another more lively motive appears: (♩ ♪♩ ♩) motive *b*. The two motives are related to each other in that both involve conjunct (stepwise) melodic movement.

Look at measures three and four. Where did they come from? What motives are they based on?

— — — — — — — — — — — — — — —

Measure three is an exact repetition of measure one (motive *a*). Similarly, measure four repeats measure two exactly (motive *b*).

Measures five through eight are basically an outgrowth of measure one. Measure one consists of notes slowly progressing *upward* by step. Except for the repeated note, measures five and six do just that: move up slowly by step. Measures seven and eight also contain slow notes moving stepwise, but the movement is *downward*. The downward movement provides variety while the slow stepwise movement keeps the musical identity of motive *a*.

Now look at measures nine and ten. As we've indicated with "*b*," these measures are a variation of motive *b*. Why do we say this? (In what way is measure nine similar to measure two?)

— — — — — — — — — — — — — — —

Measure nine has exactly the same rhythm as measure two. Also, in both measures, the notes are moving by step: again, the similar melodic contour.

Measure 2

Measure 9

(We've connected notes with a line to make the melodic contour stand out).

Now compare measures nine and ten (taken as a unit) with measures eleven and twelve. Notice that measures nine and ten have exactly the same rhythm as measures eleven and twelve. Also look at the melodic contours carefully. (Connect the notes with dots if you like.) How do the contours compare?

_ _ _ _ _ _ _ _ _ _ _ _ _ _ _

As you can see, the contours are basically the same (even though they start on different notes).

What is the name for this kind of a variation?

_ _ _ _ _ _ _ _ _ _ _ _ _ _ _

Sequence.

Frequently, in a two-part song form, the end of part one is very similar to the end of part two. Is this true in the "Sicilian Hymn"? Explain. (Compare measures seven and eight with fifteen and sixteen).

_ _ _ _ _ _ _ _ _ _ _ _ _ _ _

Yes. The contours and rhythms are exactly the same. Note that variety is provided by the use of different scale degrees.

You've just examined a two-part song form (also called a bipartite song form). But remember, a song form can have any number of parts. The two-part song form is quite common. So is the three-part (or tripartite) song form.

The Three-Part (Tripartite) Song Form

The three-part song form is characterized by a third part that returns to the melody used in the first part. If we designate part one as "A" and part two as "B," then the three-part song form would be described as ABA.

Part two is usually a clear-cut departure from part one. This way it is easy for the listener to recognize the part one melody when it returns.

The recognition of the return of part one is an important aspect of this form. To make sure that the listener doesn't forget part one, composers often repeat it immediately after it is presented, before the introduction of part two. In this case, the form would be described as: AABA. (Part one is considered to be AA, part two is B, and part three is A.) For variety, each time A is repeated, slight variations are usually introduced.

Here is an example of a three-part song form with **AABA** design. What measures make up part one? Part two? Part three?

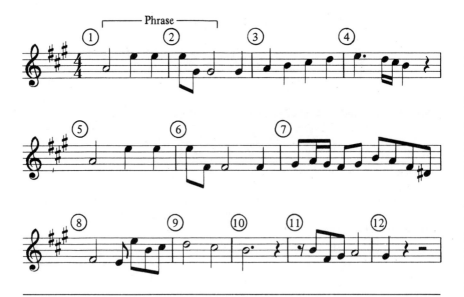

(1) The ending of part two in measure twelve leads nicely into part three. Can you explain why?

(2) Does this piece have a culmination point? If so, where is it?

(3) Does the melody have a mountain range quality?

(4) What's the melodic range?

_ _ _ _ _ _ _ _ _ _ _ _ _ _ _ _

(1) Part two ends with a leading tone, which of course *leads* nicely into the beginning note of part three, which is the tonic.

(2) Yes. The highest note is F♯″, which appears in measure fifteen and is not repeated elsewhere.

(3) Yes. The melody begins on a′, climbs up and down and finally reaches a peak at measure fifteen after which it returns to a′.

(4) The range is a major ninth (from e′ to f♯″).

Part one consists of measures one through eight. Part two includes measures nine through twelve (and also the three notes preceding measure nine). Part three is made up of measures thirteen through sixteen.

The Compound Song Form

The last degree of enlargement of melody we'll discuss is the compound song form. This is simply a combination of two or more song forms. The song form that comes first is called the *principal song*; the second one is often called the *trio*. The term *trio* was used because when these forms were first developing, the second song form was composed for three instruments or vocal parts that were to be played together. The term *trio* is still commonly used even when the second song form is not a trio in the literal sense of being written for three instruments. (Musicians, like the rest of us, sometimes keep doing things even when the original reasons for doing them are no longer valid.)

After the trio, the principal song often returns, usually with some variations. Now, suppose we designate the principal song as "A" and the "trio" as "B." What would the design be?

_ _ _ _ _ _ _ _ _ _ _ _ _

ABA. What other musical unit has the same design as the compound song form (with one trio)?

– – – – – – – – – – – – – – – – –

The three-part song form also has an **ABA** design.

Although we don't have space to go into the details of the compound song form, we will be continuing our exploration of song forms in later chapters. If you'd like to learn more about the compound song form, you may wish to study these pieces:

- Beethoven's Piano Sonata, opus 2 no. 3 (the scherzo movement)
- Schubert's Impromptu, opus 142 no. 2
- The Third Movements of Mozart's Symphones nos. 2, 3, 4, and 5

We've covered a lot in this ambitious chapter. To summarize the important points, we'll present an example of a song form and ask you a number of questions about it

Melody from Dvorak's *New World* Symphony

(Note change of clef in measure 17)

What measures make up the first part of this melody? How can you tell?

— — — — — — — — — — — — — — —

Measures one through eight make up part one. We can tell, because there is a definite cadence on e″ (the keynote) in measure eight. (The end of a part is usually marked by a definite cadence.) The rest in measure nine also helps to separate it from the previous measures, which do *not* contain any rests.

Does the melody of part one return? If so, where?

— — — — — — — — — — — — — — —

Yes, it returns in measures seventeen through twenty-three. Notice that measures seventeen through twenty-three are two octaves lower than one through eight, but that the letter names of the notes are exactly the same (except that the notes in measure six are mysteriously omitted when the part one melody returns.)

How would you describe the form of this *New World* melody? Two-part song form? Three part song form? What?

— — — — — — — — — — — — — — —

Three-part song form.

Does the *New World* melody start out with stable degrees?

— — — — — — — — — — — — — — —

Yes: The mediant and dominant

The first phrase of the melody contains two motives. Find as many measures as you can that contain each of these motives. (Remember, a motive may appear in varied form).

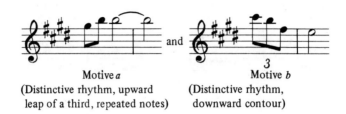

Motive *a*
(Distinctive rhythm, upward
leap of a third, repeated notes)

Motive *b*
(Distinctive rhythm,
downward contour)

Measures that contain motive *a*:
Measures that contain motive *b*:

It will take some time and effort to do this, but this type of analysis will improve your understanding of motivic variations.

— — — — — — — — — — — — — — — —

Besides the first statement of motive *a* in measures one and two, it clearly appears in measures 9, 13, 17, and 20.

- In addition, it appears in somewhat different dress in measures 6-7, 8, 9, 11-12, 13, 15-16, and 23. In measures 6-7, the notes g″ and b″ appear. These exact same pitches also appear in the first statement of the motive.
- In measures 8 and 23 the leap of a minor third appears in contrary motion (downward instead of upward). Also, notice that the rhythm is similar: (♪♪♩)
- In 9 and 13 the same contour appears but with different rhythm and different degrees.
- In 11-12 and 15-16, the same degrees are used but their *order* is switched. The rhythm is very similar to that used in the opening motivic statement.

After its opening statement in measures 2 and 3, motive *b* appears clearly in measures 10-11, 14-15, and 18-19.

- You may have noticed that in measures 10 and 14, the interval of a fourth is replaced by the interval of a third. Still, the motive is clearly recognizable because the contour and rhythm are generally preserved.
- Measures 5-6, and 21-22 also contain variations on the downward sloping contour of motive *b*, but the resemblance is less clear.

Let's finish this chapter by reviewing two important ideas that we began with:

(1) Does the new *New World* melody have a culmination point? If so, what is it?
(2) Does it have a mountain range quality?

— — — — — — — — — — — — — — —

(1) Yes: e′″ (measure 5)
(2) Yes. Like most good melodies it does have a mountain range quality, as you can see:

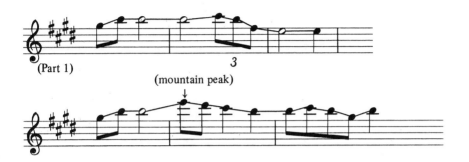

(Part 1)

(mountain peak)

(Cadence on low note)

CHAPTER EIGHT

Chords

Remember from chapter 5 that harmony refers to tones that sound simultaneously. As you learned, a harmonic interval is one in which two tones sound simultaneously. A *chord* is a combination of *three* or more simultaneously sounding tones.

In this chapter you learn about the structure of individual chords. In chapter 9 you will learn about harmonic progression—the movement of chords within a tonality or key. When you finish this chapter, you will be able to

- ● Recognize and notate each of these kinds of chords:
  - —Major, minor, diminished, and augmented triads
  - —Seventh, ninth, and thirteenth chords
  - —Quartel chords
- ● Recognize and notate:
  - —Open and close spacing of chord tones
  - —Root position and first and second inversion of chords

Chord Construction

There are various ways to make chords. We'll start with a basic approach that composers have been using since about the 17th century building chords called "triads." Later we'll show you some other approaches.

1. Pick a degree of the scale that you want to use as the foundation of the chord, that is, a degree above which you will systematically add other tones to make a chord. (This degree is commonly referred to as the *root* of the chord.)

   Let's say you're in the key of G and you want to build a chord on the tonic (so that the tonic is the root of the chord). You might start by writing a note on g' like this:

 ← Root

2. Next, you would add a tone which is a *third* above the root:

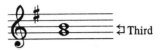 ♮ Third

3. Then, add a tone that is a *fifth* above the root.

 ♮ Fifth

That's all there is to it. The chord we have just constructed is called a *triad* because it is made up of three different scale degrees, each a third apart.

Chord Tone Names

Each tone of a chord has a name. You already know the foundation tone upon which the chord is constructed is called the *root*. The tone that is a *third* above the root is called the *third*. (Simple, right?) Similarly, the tone a fifth above the root is called the *fifth*. In this chord, which pitch is the root? Third? Fifth?

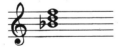

– – – – – – – – – – – – –

The root is b♭', the third d", and the fifth is f".

Now you try it. On the staff below build a triad on the dominant in the key of G-major, that is, make the dominant the root of the chord:

Let's do another one. In the key of A-major, build a triad that has the supertonic as its root.

Chord Names

The *root* and the *third* of a triad help to determine its name. The following chord is called a C-major triad because the root is c′, the "third" is a *major* third above the root, and the fifth is a *perfect* fifth.

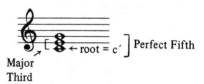

Now you try naming a chord. What is this chord called?

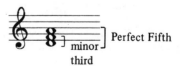

‒ ‒ ‒ ‒ ‒ ‒ ‒ ‒ ‒ ‒ ‒ ‒ ‒ .‒ ‒

D-minor triad. The root is D, and the *third* is a *minor* third above the root. (See Chapter 5 to review minor thirds).

Chord Inversions

When you first build a chord, the root is always the lowest tone. But when you use a chord in actual music this isn't always the case. The chord tones may be rearranged so that the *third* or *fifth* is the lowest tone. When the root is the lowest tone, a chord is said to be in root position. When the third is the lowest tone, the chord is said to be in the first inversion. When the fifth is the lowest tone, the chord is in the second inversion:

C-major triad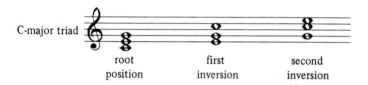

          root   first   second
         position   inversion   inversion

It's important to understand chord inversions because the quality of a chord is changed when it is put into different inversions. A chord in root position, for example, has a strong, stable sound. A chord in the first inversion sounds much "lighter," as if it wants to move on to another chord. The second inversion changes the sound of a chord quite drastically and needs to be used with care. (More on this inversion later.)

Tell whether each of these F-major triads is in root position, first inversion, or second inversion. (For an F-major triad, F is the root, A is the third and C is the fifth.)

          root
     (a)   (b)   (c)   (d)

‒ ‒ ‒ ‒ ‒ ‒ ‒ ‒ ‒ ‒ ‒ ‒ ‒ ‒

(a) root postion: the lowest tone is the root
(b) second inversion: the lowest tone is C, the *fifth* of the F-major triad
(c) and (d) first inversions: in both cases A (the third of the chord) is the lowest tone.

An easy way to change a chord from root position to first inversion is to move the root of the chord up an octave while keeping the third and fifth in the same staff position, as shown here. In the first inversion the third is the lowest note:

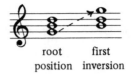

root   first
position inversion

To change a chord from first inversion to second inversion, move the third up an octave

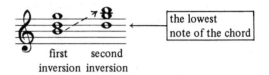

the lowest
note of the chord

first   second
inversion inversion

Change this E-minor chord to first inversion and then to second inversion:

- - - - - - - - - - - - -

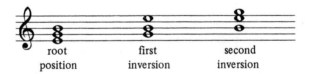

root   first   second
position   inversion   inversion

Spacing of Chord Tones

So far the chord tones of the triads we have looked at have been close together on the staff in what is called *close spacing*. For example, here is an E-minor chord in root position with close spacing.

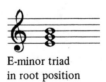

E-minor triad
in root position

But the chord tones may be spread out in what is called *open spacing*. Here is that same root position E-minor triad in open spacing.

E-minor triad
in root position

Here is another way of spacing these same chord tones in open position.

Notice that we still are using the same letter names: E, G, and B, and that E is always the lowest tone. The use of different spacings of the same chord within a composition helps to provide variety.

Spacing Guidelines

There are two important guidelines to follow in deciding how to space a chord.

- Avoid close spacing below c. Close spacing below c sounds "muddy" or like growling.

- Don't put an interval greater than an octave between any two *upper* notes. (the interval between the lower two notes can be greater than an octave.)

Which of these chord spacings follow the guidelines we just presented?

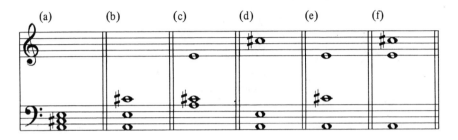

– – – – – – – – – – – – – – –

Spacings (b), (c), (e), and (f). Notice that in spacing (b) the third of the chord is moved up an octave from where it would be in close spacing. In (c) close spacing is used to good effect because the pitches are higher (well above c). In (3) there is a large interval between the lowest tone and the next to the lowest tone, but that's OK since the two upper tones are fairly close together. Spacing (f) is also in line with our guidelines since the upper two tones are within an octave of each other. Spacing (a) doesn't follow our guideline about avoiding close spacing below c. Spacing (d) is not recommended because there is more than an octave between the two upper notes. The c♯ʺ is too far from e; consequently, it sounds "thin" or unsupported. It doesn't blend well with the tone e.

Analyzing Triads

It is useful to be able to look at a triad and tell what its root is and whether it is major or minor. Once you can do this you can begin to see how a series of chords fits together. If the triad is in root position, it's easy to find the root: the lowest tone is always the root.

Recognizing Root Position

Triads in root position with close spacing are easy to recognize because each chord tone is a third above the next. Also, notice that when a triad is in root position the notes are either all on lines or all on spaces.

All chord tones   All chord tones
on lines   on spaces

Which of these chords are in the root position? (Try to work quickly, looking for chord tones "stacked" a third apart.)

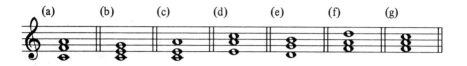

- - - - - - - - - - - - - -

Chords (b) and (g).

If a triad is not in close spacing, it's more difficult to tell whether it is in root position. Until you become more experienced in analyzing triads, it's a good idea to change any chords you see into close spacing in root position.

To do this, rearrange the notes so that they are either all on successive lines or all on successive spaces.

For example, if you see this triad:

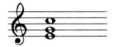

move the top note down an octave

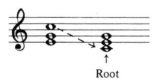

Root

Now that all three notes are on lines, the triad is in root position with close spacing and it is easy to see that the root is c'.

Following are more examples of chords in different positions and spacing. In each of these examples we have rearranged the chord tones so the chords are in root position with close spacing.

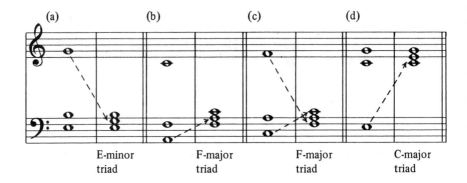

Now it's your turn. Write each of these chords in root position in close spacing *in the treble clef*. Then write the full name of each chord below the staff.

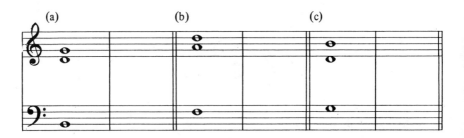

Name of chord: (a)_____ (b)_____ (c)_____

_ _ _ _ _ _ _ _ _ _ _ _ _ _ _ _ _ _

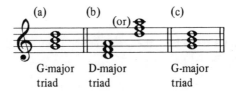

Notice that both (a) and (c) are G-major triads even though they look quite different in their original spacing and position.

Doubling of Chord Tones

A triad, as you know, is made up of three degrees. Each degree, of course, has a different letter name. But often one (or more) of the degrees is duplicated in a higher or lower octave. When this happens we say that the chord tones have been *doubled*. For example, here is a C-major triad in root position with *no* doubling:

Here is the same chord with the root and third doubled:

And here's another version of a C-major triad with extensive doubling of its chord tones:

(Key of C)

It's still called a triad since there are only three different degrees in the chord: one, three, and five. (C, E, and G in the key of C).

A triad written in root position with no doubling is sometimes referred to as the "skeleton" of a more extensive doubling of the same chord.

For each of the following chords write the skeleton in the treble clef. Then below the staff write the name of each chord.

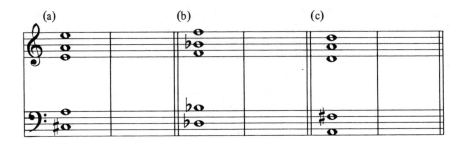

Name of chord: (a)_____ (b)_____ (c) _____

- - - - - - - - - - - - - - -

A-major triad   Bb-minor triad   D-major triad

Diminished and Augmented Triads

Most triads are either major or minor. Both major and minor triads have perfect fifths. But a *diminished* triad is triad with a *minor* third and a *diminished* fifth.

An augmented triad has a *major* third and an *augmented fifth*.

You will probably not use these chords very often (especially the augmented chord). Still it's good to have them in your chordal vocabulary because they are sometimes useful.

Here is a G-major chord. Change it to (a) a G-minor chord, (b) a G-diminished chord, and (c) a G-augmented chord.

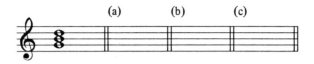

In (a) we lowered the third to make it minor. In (b) we lowered the fifth to make it diminished. In (c) we used a major third and an augmented fifth.

Seventh Chords

So far we have only been discussing triads—three note chords. You can construct a four-note chord by adding an extra tone a seventh above the *root* of the chord. Such a chord is called a seventh chord.

Change each of these triads into a seventh chord:

Notice that in (a) all these chord tones are on spaces.
Notice that in (b) all these chord tones are on lines.

Inversions of Seventh Chords

Seventh chords can be inverted just like triads. There are three inversions possible:

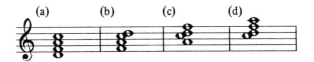

(a) Seventh chord in root position
(b) First inversion (third the lowest tone)
(c) Second inversion (fifth the lowest tone)
(d) Third inversion (seventh the lowest tone)

Here are some seventh chords in different inversions. Write the skeleton of each in the treble clef.

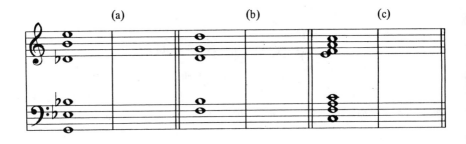

- - - - - - - - - - - - - - - -

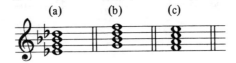

(Notice in these skeleton chords how the chord tones are stacked on all lines or all spaces.)

All three of these seventh chords have *perfect fifths* between the root and the fifth. This isn't the case with all seventh chords, however.

Another important seventh chord is the *diminished seventh* chord.

Notice that this chord has a diminished seventh, diminished fifth, and a minor third.

A related chord is the *half-diminished seventh* chord

Take a guess: why do you suppose it's called "half-diminished"?

— — — — — — — — — — — — — — —

Because it has only one diminished interval (the diminished seventh) whereas a diminished seventh chord has two diminished intervals (the diminished seventh and the diminished fifth).

Kinds of Seventh Chords

There are several different kinds of seventh chords. Some have major sevenths; some have minor sevenths. Some have major thirds; some have minor thirds. Here are three important seventh chords to know about.

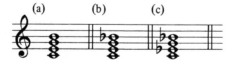

(a) Major seventh with major third; commonly referred to as a "major seventh" chord for short.
(b) Minor seventh with major third; referred to as a "seventh" chord.
(c) Minor seventh with minor third; referred to as a "minor seventh" chord.

We've covered quite a lot in the last few paragraphs. Let's pause and review the key features of the different seventh chords in a table:

Table 8-1 Seventh Chords

name of chord	chord tone		
	third	fifth	seventh
seventh	major	perfect	minor
major seventh	major	perfect	major
minor seventh	minor	perfect	minor
diminished seventh	minor	diminished	diminished
half-diminished seventh	minor	perfect	diminished

Ninth Chords

The chords you have been studying are sometimes called *tertiary* chords because each successive chord tone is the interval of a third above the previous one (*tertiary* comes from the Latin *tertiarius*, meaning "third").

We can continue this tertiary pattern and construct a five-tone chord by adding yet another tone a third above the previous chord tone.

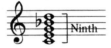

As you can see, this results in what is called a ninth chord because the interval between the root and the top chord tone is a ninth.

Often one of the chord tones of a ninth chord is omitted.

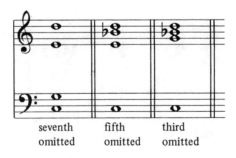

seventh	fifth	third
omitted	omitted	omitted

Construct a G ninth chord on the treble clef staff following. Use a major third, perfect fifth, minor seventh and major ninth. Don't omit any chord tones.

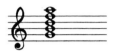

Here are some interesting chords taken from Grieg's Sonata, Opus 7. See if you can figure out what they are and match them to the descriptions given below.

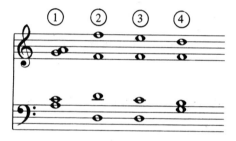

NOTE: We've written the chords in whole notes without bar lines so you can concentrate on the chords without being distracted by the rhythm.

Write the skeleton version of each chord on the staff below.

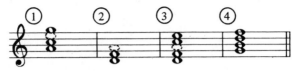

⟨:⟩ = omitted chord tone

Now match each chord description to the proper chord above. Write the number of each chord in the blank beside its description.

Chord Descriptions

_____ (a) 7th chord (with minor 7th and minor third);

_____ (b) 7th chord (with minor 7th and major third);

_____ (c) 9th chord with omitted 5th (with major 9th, minor 7th, and minor third);

_____ (d) minor triad (with 5th omitted)

Write the skeleton version of the chords from Grieg's Sonata here:

— — — — — — — — — — — — —

(a) 1   (b) 4   (c) 3   (d) 2

Eleventh Chords

The skeleton version of an eleventh chord doesn't go together well with triads and seventh chords because it contains so many dissonant intervals. That's why composers usually omit one or more tones. They may omit the third of the chord because it clashes with the eleventh. Here's an example:

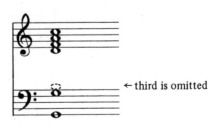

← third is omitted

Thirteenth Chords

Now see if you can construct the skeleton of a thirteenth chord that has c′ as its root (use only degrees that would occur in the key of F).

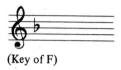

(Key of F)

- - - - - - - - - - - - - - -

As you might guess, the thirteenth chord rarely occurs with all of its chord tones intact. For example, the third and fifth may be omitted, as in this example:

Well, that about does it as far as tertiary chords are concerned. A fifteenth chord? No. That's not possible! Can you explain why?

(Try constructing one!)

- - - - - - - - - - - - - - -

A tone that is a fifteenth above the root is merely *doubling* the root. For example:

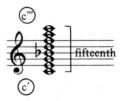

Now that you know how to construct triads, seventh, ninth, eleventh, and thirteenth chords, let's consider the shorthand system used in popular music for notating these chords.

Chord Symbols in Popular Music

Major Triads

A capital letter written above the melody indicates that a major triad in root position is to sound simultaneously with the melody. (It is understood that the chord is to continue to sound until a new chord symbol appears above the staff.)

Here's an example of how this works. Notice in the following example that a C-major triad is indicated for measure one (by the letter C) and an F-major triad, for measure two:

The rhythm and spacing of these chords is left to the discretion of the performer. Here's one possibility:

Arpeggio

Here is another way the chords might be arranged. Notice that in this example the chord tones are *not* all sounding at exactly the same time but are played in succession. This is known as an *arpeggiated* chord or an *arpeggio*.

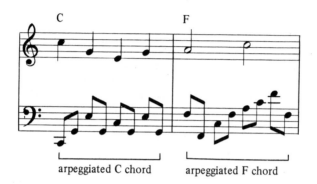

arpeggiated C chord   arpeggiated F chord

Arpeggio comes from the Italian *arpeggiare* meaning "to play on the harp."

Root Position and Inversions

The chord symbol in popular music for the major triad in *root position* is simply a capital letter. The performer may arrange the chord at his or her discretion as long as the root is kept as the lowest tone. If an inversion is desired, the letter name of the chord tone that is to be the lowest note is given in parentheses along with the word *bass*. For example, to indicate an F chord in first inversion, you would write F(A bass).

F(A bass) =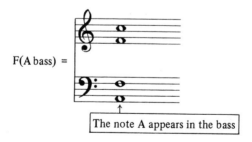

The note A appears in the bass

A similar system is used for the other chords you have learned. Let's consider each of them one at a time.

Minor Triads

A capital letter followed by a lower-case "m" indicates a minor triad. For example, "Em" means "E-minor triad."

Diminished Triads

Diminished triads are indicated by a capital letter plus "dim" written in lower case letters:

Seventh Chords

As you will recall there are different kinds of seventh chords. The chord commonly referred to as a "seventh chord" (which has a major third and minor seventh) is indicated by simply adding a "7" to the capital letter.

A major seventh chord (which has a major third and major seventh) is indicated by writing a capital letter followed by "maj7."

A minor seventh chord (a seventh chord with a minor third and a minor seventh) is written with a capital letter, a lower case "m" and "7."

Dm7 =

A seventh chord with a minor third, diminished fifth, and diminished seventh (called a diminished seventh chord) is indicated by writing "dim7" after the capital letter.

Fdim7 =

Write the skeleton version of each of these chords using whole notes:

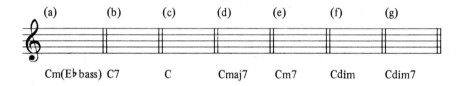

(a)	(b)	(c)	(d)	(e)	(f)	(g)
Cm(Eb bass)	C7	C	Cmaj7	Cm7	Cdim	Cdim7

– – – – – – – – – – – – – – – – – –

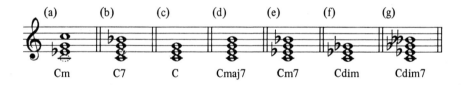

(a)	(b)	(c)	(d)	(e)	(f)	(g)
Cm	C7	C	Cmaj7	Cm7	Cdim	Cdim7

(1) For the following chords, identify the Em7 chord(s).
(2) Which are arpeggiated chords?

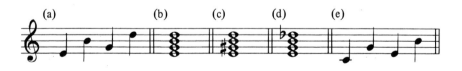

– – – – – – – – – – – – – – – – – –

(1) Both (a) and (b) are Em7 chords.
(2) Both (a) and (e) are arpeggiated chords (or arpeggios).

Ninth Chords

Unless indicated otherwise, ninth chords in popular music have major thirds, *minor* sevenths, and *major* ninths. The symbol is a capital letter plus "9."

Eleventh and Thirteenth Chords

Eleventh and thirteenth chords are both written with a capital letter plus the appropriate number (11 or 13).

Notice that a perfect eleventh and major thirteenth are used in these chords.

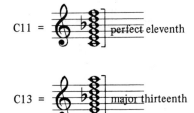

Ear Training

So far, you've learned how to build a lot of different chords. But you may not have heard them. If possible, we suggest you play all of the musical illustrations in this chapter, listening carefully to the sound of the various chords in their different spacings and inversions. You may wish to order an audiotape for self-study to develop an ear for chords. See the Appendix.

Optional Exercises

Play each of these chords on an instrument and listen carefully. Then see if you can match each chord to the adjective that best describes it.

Chords	Adjectives
_____ (1) A-major	a. sad, pensive
_____ (2) B♭-minor	b. sweet (romantic)
_____ (3) Cmaj7	c. bright
_____ (4) Fdim7	d. dramatic (energetic)

— — — — — — — — — — — — — — —

This exercise is highly subjective. But still most musicians that we asked agreed with these answers:

(1) c   (2) a   (3) b   (4) d

Here's another similar question. This time we will notate the chords. Give it a try, remembering that there are no dogmatic rules or clearly right answers.

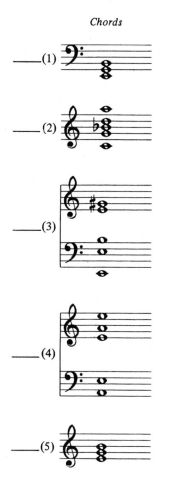

Chords	Adjectives
	a. sad
	b. romantic
	c. empty, lean
	d. rumbly and stable
	e. warm, rich

— — — — — — — — — — — — — — — —

(1) d: Any chords this low in pitch tend to sound "muddy," "growly," or "rumbly."

(2) b: Many agree that major ninth and thirteenth chords have a "romantic" sound. They often appear in popular slow ballads.

(3) e: We think this E-major triad sounds "warm and rich." This is probably because the chord tones dovetail with the overtones of the lowest note. (More on this in the next chapter.)

(4) c: This isn't really a traditional chord as it has only two tones. It sounds empty because it is missing the *third*.

(5) a: We think "sad" is the best adjective for the E-minor chord. Minor chords are often described as having a somber or pensive quality. But compare this chord with (1), which is also an E-minor chord.

Newer Approaches to Chord Construction

What you have learned so far about tertiary chord construction is applicable to nearly all popular music written today. Yet this approach to building chords is more than 200 years old! Some twentieth century composers, in their search for new sounds, have been experimenting with different approaches to chord construction. One new approach is to use a different interval as the basis for chord construction (say, a *fourth* instead of a *third*).

Quartel Chords

Chords built on fourths are known as *quartel chords*. Usually perfect fourths are used. Here are some examples:

Since most of you are used to hearing only tertiary chords, quartel chords may sound quite strange. Composers often use quartel chords when they are writing background music for movie scenes depicting trips into outerspace or other futuristic adventures.

Chords Built From Fifths

Perfect fifths can also be stacked on top of each other to create new chords. Recall that when the interval of a fourth is inverted, it becomes a fifth. An interval that results from an inversion has a sound similar to the original interval. So perfect fifth chords sound quite a lot like quartel chords. Here are some examples:

All the chord construction methods we have looked at so far involve stacking a given interval. To create the traditional tertiary chords, we stacked *thirds*. You've seen how new chords can also be created by stacking other intervals such as perfect fourths and fifths.

Another approach is to freely combine any tones of the scale without consistently stacking any given interval. For example, suppose you are using this six-note scale:

You might choose to combine E, D, and G to produce this triad (a); or you might want to combine A, B, and C as in (b):

(a)   (b)

Using this system, you carefully analyze each chord and note the intervals formed by the combination of chord tones. For example, the triad containing the tones C, D, and G would be called "p2s" since it contains two perfect intervals and a major second. ("p" in this system stands for "perfect" and "s" for major second.) The A-B-C chord would be called an "nsd" chord since it contains a minor third, and a major and minor second. (n = minor third; s = major second; d = minor second, dissonant interval.)

Further discussion of these new approaches to chord construction is beyond the scope of this book. For more details, we suggest you refer to *Harmonic Materials of Modern Music* by Howard Hanson and *Twentieth Century Harmony* by Vincent Persichetti.

In this chapter, we have covered a lot about chords, so we will conclude this discussion with a few review questions so you can check your understanding of the main ideas in the chapter.

(1) Rewrite these chords in skeleton form in the treble clef given below. Then give the

popular music symbols for each chord.

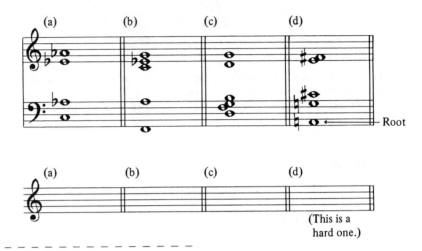

(This is a
hard one.)

- - - - - - - - - - - - - -

For questions (2) through (5) tell whether each of the chords in question (1) is in the root positions, or first, second, or third inversion. Check the correct answer.

(2) Chord *a* is in
_____ (a) Root position
_____ (b) First inversion
_____ (c) Second inversion
_____ (d) Third inversion

(3) Chord *b* is in
_____ (a) Root position
_____ (b) First inversion
_____ (c) Second inversion
_____ (d) Third inversion

(4) Chord *c* is in
_____ (a) Root position
_____ (b) First inversion
_____ (c) Second inversion
_____ (d) Third inversion

(5) Chord *d* is in
_____ (a) Root position
_____ (b) First inversion
_____ (c) Second inversion
_____ (d) Third inversion

(6) Which chord tones, if any, are doubled in chord *c* in question (1)?

(7) Does chord *a* illustrate open or closed spacing?

(8) Which of these is a quartel chord?

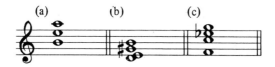

(9) Write a skeleton version of each of these chords:

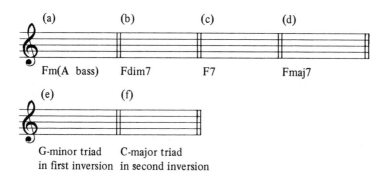

Fm(A bass)   Fdim7   F7   Fmaj7

G-minor triad   C-major triad
in first inversion in second inversion

- - - - - - - - - - - - - - - -

(1)   (a)   (b)   (c)   (d)

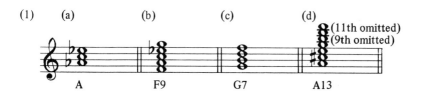

(11th omitted)
(9th omitted)

A   F9   G7   A13

(2) (b): First inversion
(3) (a): Root position
(4) (c): Second inversion
(5) (a): Root position
(6) The fifth and root
(7) Open spacing
(8) Chord *a*

(9)

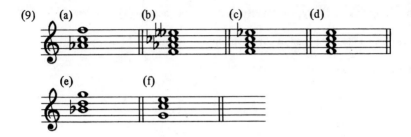

CHAPTER NINE

Chord Progression and Harmonization

In the last chapter you learned about the structure and sound of individual chords. This chapter deals with the progression or movement from one chord to another. In tonal music certain successions of chords seem to sound "strong" and "make sense," whereas other progressions have a "weak" or "soft" effect. You'll learn some simple guidelines in this chapter that will enable you to construct strong chord progressions. You'll also learn to harmonize a melody; that is, you'll learn to construct a chord progression that will go together well with an existing melody. More specifically, when you finish this chapter, you'll be able to

- Give the degree names for various chords
- Identify and construct strong chord progressions
- Treat a melody note as either a chord tone or nonharmonic tone when harmonizing a melody
- Notate harmonic rhythm
- Harmonize a melody₁ with a strong chord progression making use of harmonic and nonharmonic tones

To construct chord progressions and harmonize melodies, it's crucial to understand that chords have degree names.

Degree Names for Chords

As you learned in chapter 8, the root of a chord is the basis for its name. A major triad with A as its root may be called A-major. But chords also have degree names as well as letter names, since we can build a triad on each of the degrees of the scale. (That is, each degree can be the root of a triad.)

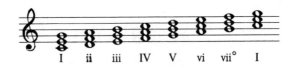

I   ii   iii   IV   V   vi   vii°   I

On the degrees of the C-major scale, for example, we can build these triads.

As you can see, we use Roman numerals to show the degree designation for each chord. Notice, too, that we use lowercase to show that a triad is minor and uppercase to show that it is major. A degree symbol (°) shows that a triad is diminished.

In the major scale, as shown in the previous figure, which triads are major? (Show your answer with Roman numerals.) Major?_____ Minor?_____ Diminished?_____

— — — — — — — — — — — — — — — —

Major: I, IV, V;   Minor: ii, iii, vi;   Diminished: vii°

Minor Scale Triads

Here are the triads for the natural minor scale:

Key of A-minor

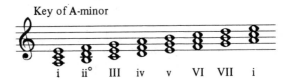

i   ii°   III   iv   v   VI   VII   i

Examine the natural minor triads.
Which are minor? _____ Major? _____ Diminished? _____

— — — — — — — — — — — — — — — —

Minor: i, iv, v;   Major: III, VI, VII;   Diminished: ii°

The Harmonic Minor

Notice that the triad on the dominant (5th degree) in the natural minor scale is minor. Usually, this triad is *not* used, but is replaced with a major triad of the harmonic minor scale. That is because, as you may remember from earlier chapters, the raised seventh degree provides a more powerful pull upward to the tonic.

Key: A (harmonic) minor

Which of these is a V chord for a harmonic minor scale?

Key: G-minor   Key: F-minor   Key: F♯-minor

Both (a) and (b) are; (c) is a v (minor), not a V.

Identify these chords by giving the Roman numeral degree designation for each:

(Major key)   (Minor key)   (Major key)   (Minor key)

(a) ii   (b) iv   (c) V   (d) i

It's important to think of the degree names of chords (v, IV, or iii) rather than just their letter names (F, G, etc.). Certain kinds of chord progressions tend to occur again and again in various keys or tonalities. It's relatively easy to learn to recognize these progressions if you think of the degree names of the chords, but difficult if you focus on letter names. For example, do any of the chords listed below look the same to you? Probably not unless you're an experienced musician:

    a) Dm - F - B♭ - Gm - A - Dm.
    b) C - Em - Am - F - G - C.
    c) E - G♯m - C♯m - A - B - E.
    d) A - F♯m - Bm - E - D - A.

But now, let's rewrite these same chords using their degree names.

a) Key of D minor: i III VI iv V i.
b) Key of C: I iii vi IV V I.
c) Key of E: I iii vi IV V I.
d) Key of A: I vi ii V IV I.

1. Which chord progressions are *basically* the same?
2. Is it easier to tell this from the letter names or degree names?

— — — — — — — — — — — — — —

1. Progressions (a), (b), and (c) are basically the same. (a) is in a minor key but the progression of degree roots is the same.
2. Your choice. Most agree that the use of degree names or numbers makes it much easier to recognize the similarity in the chord progressions.

Another advantage to using degree names is that we can teach you some guidelines for composing chord progressions. These guidelines will apply no matter what key the music is written in.

GUIDELINES FOR CHORD PROGRESSIONS

Chord progressions are sometimes categorized as "strong" or "weak." A strong progression is dynamic and gives the impression that the music is surging forward. A weak progression has a soft effect. When used (not very often in classical music), it tends to coincide with a movement from a strong to a weak beat.

For now, when you are doing the exercises in this book, we suggest you stick to strong chord progressions. Later you can experiment with weak progressions when you gain more experience.

Recognizing and Constructing Strong Progressions

It's relatively easy to recognize and construct a strong chord progression. Here are a few guidelines.

1. A strong chord progression is strong if the root of the first chord moves
   ● down a fifth (or up a fourth)
   ● up a second (or down a seventh)
   ● down a third (or up a sixth)
   to the root of the next chord.

NOTE: The inversions of these root movements are also considered strong. The most common is the inversion of *down* a *fifth* to *up* a *fourth*.

2. Any chord following the tonic chord creates a strong chord progression because of the effect of moving away from the tonic or "home base."

3. The progression IV- I is strong.

Here are some examples of strong chord progressions in the key of C

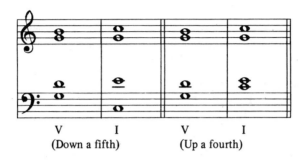

V   I   V   I
(Down a fifth)   (Up a fourth)

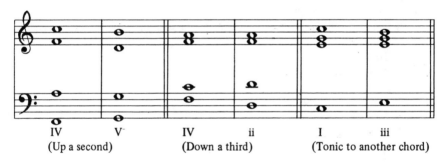

IV   V⁻   IV   ii   I   iii
(Up a second) (Down a third) (Tonic to another chord)

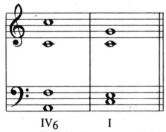

IV₆   I
(Subdominant to tonic)
(Note: in this example the "6" after the "IV" shows that the IV chord is in first inversion.)

Now let's apply these guidelines. Identify the strong chord progression(s):

  a) I–iii
  b) V–IV
  c) iii–V

— — — — — — — — — — — — — —

In (b) the progression goes down a second. In (c) the progression is up a third. In (a) the root movement is also up a third, but the progression is still strong because it starts with the tonic chord.

Now let's apply these guidelines to some examples where we're dealing with chords by letter name. Which of these (or parts of these) are strong chord progressions? (Hint: translate the letter names of the chords to degree names before evaluating the progressions.)

   a) Key of A-minor: Am C F Dm
   b) Key of G-major: D7 C Em D7
   c) Key of C: F Dm Em C

— — — — — — — — — — — — — —

(a) (c):
In (a) the progressions are all strong:
  ● i to III, tonic to mediant (any chord following the tonic makes a strong progression.)
  ● III to VI (down a fifth)
  ● VI to iv (down a third)

In (c) the strong progressions are:
  ● Down a third (IV to ii)
  ● Up a second (ii to iii)
  ● Down a third (iii to I)

In (b) the progressions are weak because they are:
  ● Down a second (V7 to IV)
  ● Up a third (IV to vi)
  ● Down a second (vi to V7)

A knowledge of strong chord progressions can be useful when writing music, if you know where you want to start and end but aren't sure where you want to go in between. Often it's desirable to start a phrase with a tonic chord and end it with a dominant chord. The tonic chord would make a firm start, and the dominant chord at the end would create tension and prepare the way for the second phrase. Let's say that we want to use one chord per measure and that we are writing a four-measure phrase. What would we put in measures two and three?

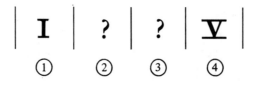

A good chord to use in measure three is ii because the ii–V progression is strong (down a fifth). What other chords might we use in measure three?

— — — — — — — — — — — — — — —

IV or I
- IV would be good because IV–V is strong (up a second).
- I is correct because I can precede any chord.
- VII° is not OK because it is a diminished chord; its use is best avoided except in special cases.

So we could use either ii, IV, or I. Let's suppose we're in the mood for a minor chord, so we pick ii. Now, what might we use for measure two?

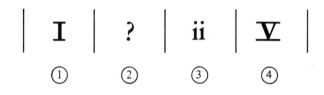

— — — — — — — — — — — — — — —

vi, IV, or I

Let's try another one. Suppose you have decided to use these chords:

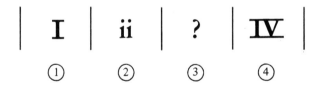

The problem is what chord should you use in measure three? This is a rather tough one. See if you can work it out on your own. Or, if you like, just check out our analysis below.

— — — — — — — — — — — — — — —

One approach is to list first the chords that could precede the IV chord (without regard for the chord in measure two)—I, iii, or vi—and then pick out those that may follow ii. We can rule out the I chord, because the progression ii–I is weak (down a second), and the vi chord, because the progression ii–vi is also weak (up a fifth). This leaves the iii chord, which works well because ii–iii is strong (up a second).

Fill in the appropriate chords in the progressions problems given here. In each item tell what chord(s) could be used where there is a box. Use only strong chord progressions. Do *not* use vii°.

Example: I V ☐ ii
I or vi

  (a) I ☐ vi IV ☐ I
  (b) I ☐ IV ☐ iii

_ _ _ _ _ _ _ _ _ _ _ _ _ _ _ _

(a) iii or V, V
(b) vi or iii, V

Now that you can recognize and construct strong chord progressions, you're ready to learn how to harmonize melody.

Harmonizing a Melody

Suppose you have a melody and you want to put some chords with it to make it sound richer and fuller. That's called harmonization.

The first step in harmonizing a melody is to determine which triads are available for use with each melody note. Usually, for a given melody note there are three triads that can be used to harmonize it. That's because each melody note can be either the root, third, or fifth of a triad. For example in a C-major melody, G can be the fifth of the I chord, the root of a V chord, the third of a iii chord, or the fifth of a I chord. Similarly, the sixth degree can be the root of a vi chord, the third of a IV chord and the fifth of a ii chord.

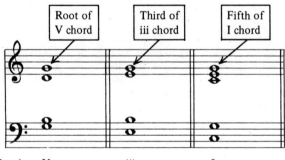

Key: C-major   V   iii   I

This table summarizes the triads that can be used to harmonize each of the degrees of the scale.

Table 9-1

degree	triads for harmonizing degree
1 (8)	I, vi, IV
2	ii, "vii°," V
3	iii, I, vi
4	IV, ii, "vii°"
5	V, iii, I
6	vi, IV, ii
7	"vii°," V, iii

Note: We put vii° in quotes because it is best to avoid the vii° triad unless you are an advanced student of harmony.

What chords could be used to harmonize this melody note? Use Roman numerals to show your answer.

Key: E-major _____

– – – – – – – – – – – – – – –

iii (B as third), I (B as fifth), V (B as root)

When harmonizing a series of melody notes, it's a good idea to write the possible triads like this:

Key: G-major

Now you try it. Below each melody note, write the Roman numerals for the triads that could be used to harmonize it. We've done the first one for you.

```
I   __  __  __  __  __  __      __  __  __  __  __  __
vi  __  __  __  __  __  __      __  __  __  __  __  __
IV  __  __  __  __  __  __      __  __  __  __  __  __
```

```
I    V    iv  "vii°"  I    iii   ii     I    IV   iii    ii     I   "vii°"  I
vi   iii   IV   V     vi    I   "vii°"   vi    ii    I  "vii°"  vi    V     vi
IV   I     ii  iii    IV   vi    V      IV  "vii°"  vi    V     IV   iii    IV
```

(Again, the "vii°" triad is in quotes to remind you that it's best to avoid this diminished triad in your first efforts at harmonization.)

After you determine which chords you might choose to harmonize each note, you can create a chord progression (circle the Roman numerals you choose). For example, for the first two measures you might use:

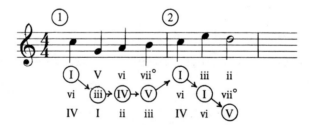

```
    I    V    vi   vii°    I    iii    ii
    vi   iii  IV    V      vi    I    vii°
    IV   I    ii   iii     IV   vi     V
```

Notice: (1) these are all strong progressions; (2) it is OK to repeat the same chord. (I is used for the first two notes in the second measure.)

Now finish the harmonization in measures three and four *using only strong progressions*. End with the tonic chord preceded by the dominant.

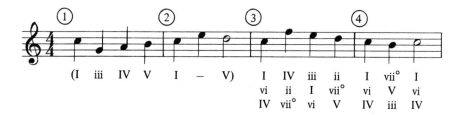

(I	iii	IV	V	I	–	V)

I	IV	iii	ii	I	vii°	I
vi	ii	I	vii°	vi	V	vi
IV	vii°	vi	V	IV	iii	IV

- - - - - - - - - - - - - - - -

There are two possible answers:

(a) I IV I V   I V I
or
(b) vi IV I V   I V I

Following the V triad in measure two, you have two possibilities. You can either go to a I (down a fifth) or a vi (up a second). If you go to I, your next chord must be a IV. (Why? Because your only other choices are ii and vii°; vii° is out because it is a diminished chord. If you try to go to ii, then your only choice after that is iii. Once you reach iii you are stuck because the only choices after iii are ii, vii°, and V, none of which are OK for a strong progression.) After IV the only chord available is I. After I you might consider going to ii, but looking ahead you can see that after it there would be no strong progression.

Now you can harmonize a melody using one chord for every melody note. This is good practice when you are learning. Your piece will probably come out sounding like a hymn, which is fine if that is the effect you want. If you want to create a different effect you need to learn how to use fewer chords, say one or two chords per measure. To do this effectively you need to know about "harmonic" and "nonharmonic" tones, which you'll do shortly. But first, write a four-measure melodic phrase with harmony according to these specifications:

- Key of A-major
- Melody using only chord tones
- One chord per measure (as indicated)
- Melody starting on the fifth degree (e′) on the last beat of the measure
- Quarter notes and half notes as indicated, except for the last note, which is to be a dotted half note
- Melodic rhythm (as indicated) ♩ | ♩ ♩ | ♩ ♩ | ♩ ♩ ♩ | ♩.

(more specifications on next page)

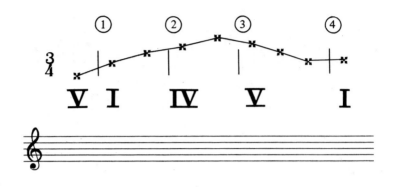

Simultaneous Melodies

In the examples that follow, you will be learning about *nonharmonic* tones. But first let's take a look at how we write several melodies at once. In standard four-part harmony, based on four voices—soprano, alto, tenor, and bass—notes on the top line have stems that go up. The melody just below the soprano is often called the alto line. The alto line is indicated in the G-clef with notes that have their stems down. A similar system is used to show the stems of tenor (notes go up) and bass (notes go down) in the F-clef. Here's an example:

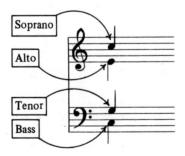

NONHARMONIC TONES

A nonharmonic tone is a tone that is not a chord tone. For example, let's say that we are using a V chord in the key of C-major. What are the chord tones of the V triad? (Give the letter names.) ___ ___ ___

_ _ _ _ _ _ _ _ _ _ _ _ _ _ _

G, B, D

Now let's suppose that instead of using the tone B in the soprano line we substitute the tone C. Since C is not a chord tone, we refer to it as a nonharmonic tone. Here's what this might look like in notation:

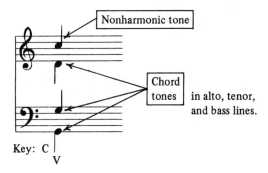

Over the years composers of traditional tonal music have developed a number of guidelines for using nonharmonic tones. By following these guidelines it's possible to use nonharmonic tones to good advantage so that they add a kind of "flavoring" to music without sounding obtrusive or out of place.

Kinds of Nonharmonic Tones

In developing the guidelines we just mentioned, composers have given names to different nonharmonic tones based on the way they are used with harmonic tones. Here are the names of the nonharmonic tones you will be learning in this chapter:

Passing tone
Neighboring tone
Suspension
Appoggiatura
Echapée (escape tone)
Anticipation

Passing Tones

Passing tones are nonharmonic tones that occur when a melody moves *stepwise* from one chord tone to another chord tone.

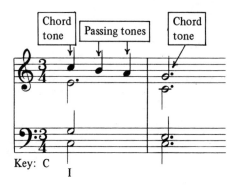

Key: C   I

Passing tones are always surrounded by chord tones. Also, they are always approached and left by stepwise motion. Here's another example:

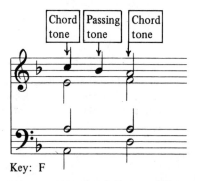

Key: F

The passing tone b♭′ is approached by a step from the chord tone c″. The b♭′ is also left by a step.

In this next example there are three passing tones. Label each one with the abbreviation PT. (Hint: Don't just look at the soprano melody.)

Key: C   I   —   I₆   IV   I

Note: I6 means "first inversion of I chord."

_ _ _ _ _ _ _ _ _ _ _ _ _ _ _ _ _

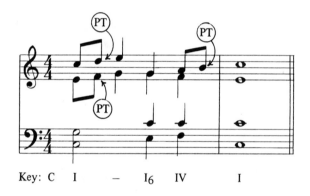

Key: C   I   —   I₆   IV   I

Here is a melody. Add some passing tones to it by changing the rhythm of this measure to

I   IV

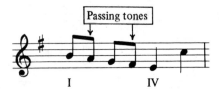

Now use your knowledge of passing tones to harmonize this phrase. Use only one chord per measure. Identify each note as either a chord tone (T) or a passing tone (PT). (We have labeled some of the nonharmonic tones and chords tones to help you.)

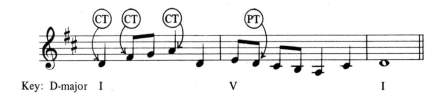

Key: D-major   I   V   I

Our next nonharmonic tone is similar to the passing tone in that it is also approached and left by a step. It's called a neighboring tone.

Neighboring Tone

A neighboring tone is a nonharmonic tone that is next to a harmonic tone in the scale. It differs from a passing tone in that it does not pass on to a new chord tone, but *returns* to the chord tone from which it was approached.

In this example, label each neighboring tone NT and each passing tone PT.

Key: C-major   IV   I

- - - - - - - - - - - -

(1) It's your turn. Using quarter notes in measure one, add an *upper* neighboring tone. Repeat the chord tone, and then add a passing tone.

- - - - - - - - - - - -

(2) Harmonize the notes in the following example, treating one of the notes as a neighboring tone and one as a passing tone.

- Use one chord per measure.
- Label the chord tones CT and nonharmonic tones either neighboring tone (NT) or passing tone (PT).

Use either a strong chord progression or use the same chord in both measures.

Key: C-major

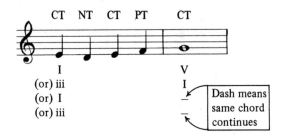

Suspension

The suspension is another nonharmonic tone. It is interesting because it shows the care with which early composers introduced nonharmonic tones.

To introduce a suspension, you first treat a melody note as a chord tone—you harmonize it with its own chord, as usual. Then you change to a new chord, but instead of moving all the chord tones together, you *hold* (suspend) the melody tone while the three other tones change. Finally, you move (resolve) the suspended melody tone to a tone of the new chord. The suspended melody tone must resolve downward a half step or a whole step.

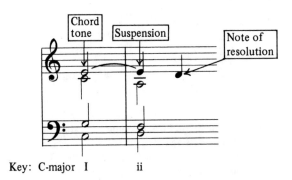

Key: C-major   I   ii

Usually the suspension occurs on an accented beat as in the above illustration.

Label each of the melodic tones in this examples as CT (chord tone), PT (passing tone), NT (neighboring tone), or S (suspension).

Key: G-major   I   V

- - - - - - - - - - - - - - - -

Key: G-major   I   V

(1) Now it's your turn again. Write a suspension following these specifications:

- Key: A-major
- Harmonic progression: I V (write the symbols below the staff).
- Melodic line: Third of tonic chord (c♯″) moves to root of tonic chord (a′). The root is sustained and becomes a suspension, which resolves to third of dominant chord
- Melodic rhythm (two measures)

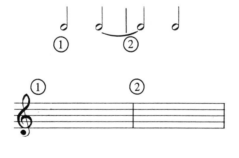

- - - - - - - - - - - - - - - -

(2) Harmonize the following notes according to these specifications:

- Key: E-minor
- Harmonic rhythm: One chord per measure (No hints this time; think of all the possibilities and choose strong progressions.)
- Melodic line: Use one passing tone and one suspension
- Label each tone as either CT, PT, or S.

(Hint: What chord is suggested by a raised seventh degree?)

- - - - - - - - - - - - - - -

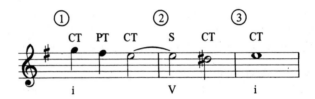

Note: The raise seventh degree suggests a V chord of a minor key. The only place for the suspension is the note e″ in measure two, and it must first be harmonized as a chord tone in measure one. The only chord that will harmonize e″ and provide a strong progression to V is i.

Appoggiatura

The *appoggiatura* is similar to the suspension in that it occurs on an accented beat and usually resolves by moving downward by step. But the appoggiatura differs in that it is approached by leap (disjunct motion).

The following example from "And I Love Her" by John Lennon and Paul McCartney contains two nonharmonic tones. Label each melody note using the abbreviations as necessary:

CT = Chord tone
AP = Appoggiatura
PT = Passing tone
NT = Neighboring tone
S = Suspension

I give her all my love
Key: D-minor   iv   i

– – – – – – – – – – – –

CT PT CT AP CT CT

I give her all my love
Key: D-minor   iv   i

Now try your hand at harmonizing these notes according to these specifications:

- Key: A-minor
- Nonharmonic tones: Use one neighboring tone and one appoggiatura.
- Harmonic rhythm: Use one chord per measure.

Note: in minor keys the tonic and subdominant chords are *minor* and are written as lower case i and iv respectively.

You might have tried one of these harmonizations:

I	IV
I	vi
I	ii
iii	IV
iii	vi
vi	—
vi	ii
vi	IV

Now this time write the melody to these specifications:

- Key: A-minor
- Chord progression: i V
- Melody:

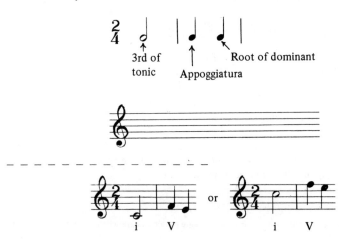

As you've learned, the appoggiatura occurs on an accented beat and is approached by a leap and left by a step. Now let's consider a nonharmonic tone that's handled in just the opposite way: the escape tone.

The Escape Tone (Echapée)

The escape tone occurs on an unaccented beat and is approached by a step and left by a leap. It's like a neighboring tone except that it does not return to the chord tone from which it is approached, but "escapes" with a leap to another chord tone.

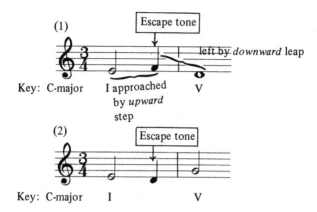

Usually the escape tone is left in the opposite direction from which it is approached. In example (1) above, the escape tone is approached by *upward* conjunct motion and left by *downward* disjunct motion.

How is the escape tone approached and left in example (2)?

— — — — — — — — — — — — — — — —

It's approached by *downward* conjunct motion and left by *upward* disjunct motion.

Now see if you can spot the escape tone and other nonharmonic tones in this example. Label each note as CT, PT, ET (escape tone), or NT.

— — — — — — — — — — — — — — — —

Anticipation

An anticipation is an advance sounding of a chord tone. Suppose a melody goes like this:

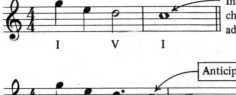

Instead of waiting to sound this chord tone here, we can sound it in advance and then repeat it, like this:

Anticipation

Label the chord tones, and anticipation, as well as the other nonharmonic tones in this example (use the abbreviation A for anticipation):

Key: F-Major   I   V   I   IV

- - - - - - - - - - - - - - - - - -

Key: F-Major   I   V   I   IV

Use your knowledge of anticipations to write a two-bar phrase according to these requirements:

- Chords: I-V
- Melody: Start with fifth of I. Leap up to third of I. Leap down to keynote. Anticipate the leading tone (3rd of V).
- Use this rhythm:

- - - - - - - - - - - - - - - -

I   –   V

Here is a melody that has been partly harmonized. (Some, but not all, of the chords are shown with Roman numerals.) Write the appropriate chord symbols on the lines given. Use only strong chord progressions.

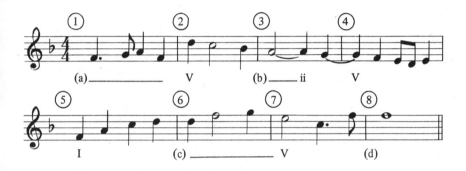

(a) _____ V   (b) ____ ii   V

I   (c) _____ V   (d)

- - - - - - - - - - - - - - - -

(a) I. It's best to start with a tonic chord. The only other chord possible is vi. But vi-V is

(b) We prefer vi. I is also possible, but we just heard I in measure one.

(c) IV. vi is a conceivable choice but not if you stick to strong progressions since our next chord is V (vi-V is weak).

(d) Use I if you want to give the phrase a feeling of finality. Use vi if you want to keep the listener up in the air waiting for more. iii is also possible but not likely. V usually progresses to I or vi. A iii chord here would also sound incomplete—but that's OK if that's the effect you want. (V–iii is a strong progression, too.)

Now go back and identify chord tones and nonharmonic tones. Label each tone as one of these: CT, AP, PT, S, NT, ET, A.

OK, you're on your own! See if you can harmonize "Auld Lang Syne." Leave C, the first note, unharmonized if you wish. Indicate your choice of chords with Roman numerals. We suggest that you use only one chord per measure, except in measure seven, where we suggest you use two chords.

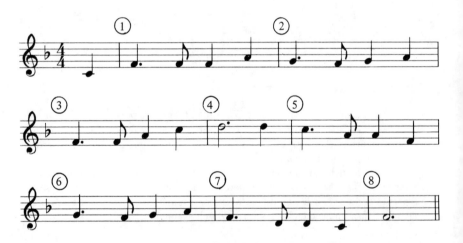

Here's one possible harmoniziation. (Yours may be different.) We've indicated the non-harmonic tones as well as the chords.

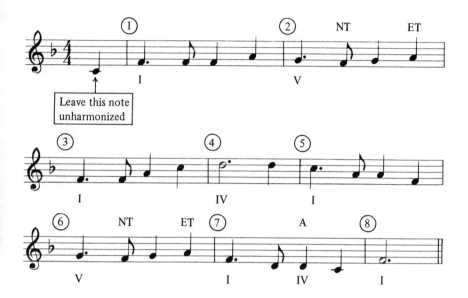

If possible, try out your harmonization with a guitar or keyboard instrument. What sounds good to you is what counts!

So far you have been harmonizing everything using only three-tone chords (triads) and nonharmonic tones. It's also possible to introduce seventh chords and ninth chords, to add color to your harmonizations.

Using Seventh Chords

A seventh can be added to any of the triads you have learned. But it's important to realize that the addition of a seventh adds dissonance and an element of tension to the sound of a chord.

In which of these places in a song do you think it would be appropriate to use a seventh chord?

    (a) The last chord
    (b) Immediately before the last tonic chord
    (c) The first chord

_ _ _ _ _ _ _ _ _ _ _ _ _ _ _ _

Actually, composers have used seventh chords in all of these places! (a) is not appropriate if you want a strong, solid feeling at the end of a song. (b) is good because the tension created by the seventh chord makes the tonic sound even more stable. (c) is not so appropriate since it's usually a good idea to begin a song with a stable tonic chord.

Often a seventh is added to the dominant triad. It is then called a "dominant seventh chord," often notated as V_7, and written:

Key: G-major V_7

The added seventh increases the tension of the V chord and makes it have an even stronger pull toward the tonic. How would this chord be indicated in popular music chord notation?

    (a) D7
    (b) Dm7
    (c) Dmaj7

_ _ _ _ _ _ _ _ _ _ _ _ _ _ _ _

D7: Notice that the V_7 chord has a major third and a *minor* seventh.

It's a little easier to harmonize melodies when you make use of seventh chords because there are four chord tones to work with instead of just three. For example, let's say we want to use one chord per measure in this melody.

I   V   I

What chord could we use for measure three? The answer (V_7) is easy if you realize that d' is the root of the dominant chord and c" is the seventh. Seventh chords are especially strong when the root of the seventh chord moves down a fifth. A V_7 chord is also predictable; it nearly always goes to I. Another effective seventh chord progression is up a second. The progression V_7–vi provides a pleasant change from the "predictable" V_7–I.

Now let's examine all of the different kinds of seventh chords as they appear in the major scale without alteration. We'll use to key of C:

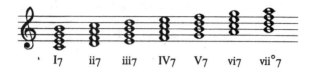

I_7 ii_7 iii_7 IV_7 V_7 vi_7 $vii°_7$

(1) Which chord(s) has (have) a major third and a minor seventh?

(2) A major third and major seventh?
(3) A minor third and minor seventh?
(4) A minor third, a diminished fifth and minor seventh?

‒ ‒ ‒ ‒ ‒ ‒ ‒ ‒ ‒ ‒ ‒ ‒ ‒ ‒ ‒

(1) V_7 (2) I_7, IV_7 (3) ii_7, iii_7, vi_7 (4) $vii°_7$

Use of Seventh Chords

Often it's effective to use a suspension with a V_7 chord so that the note of resolution is the third of the V_7 chord.

IV V_7 I

In popular music this version of the V_7 chord in the key of C would be indicated as:
G7sus
Here, "sus" is an abbreviation for suspension.

The other seventh chords, such as I_7, ii_7, iii_7, etc., are often referred to as nondominant seventh chords because they have an entirely different sound and purpose. The purpose of the V7 is to strengthen the tonic chord. The V7 has a strong pull to the tonic. Non-dominant seventh chords often have a rather "bittersweet" or "romantic" sound. Their purpose is to add color rather than to strengthen the harmonic pull to the tonic. The ii7, iii7, and vi7 chords have a slightly softer sound than the I7 and IV7 chords, perhaps because they use a minor seventh rather than the more dissonant major seventh interval. Songs, like "Evergreen" by Barbra Streisand and "Alfie" by Burt Bacharrach make heavy use of nondominant sevenths.

Ninth, Eleventh, and Thirteenth Chords

These chords may be thought of as variations on the seventh chord. Any time a seventh chord works, a ninth, eleventh, or thirteenth chord will also be likely to work. Often the decision to use one of these chords comes from the melody. For example, suppose the melody goes like this:

Key: C-major   I

Let's say you want to use a tonic chord in measure two. You also want a dominant chord in measure one so that you can have a strong V–I progression.

But e′ is not a chord tone of the V triad. However, it is a chord tone of the V13 chord. Hence, you might harmonize the notes like this:

V13   I7

Keeping in mind what you've just learned about seventh, ninth, eleventh, and thirteenth chords, harmonize "Auld Lang Syne" again. This time throw in some seventh chords where they seem appropriate. Consider using the progression V7–vi7. Also, see if you can find a place where the melody suggests a V9 chord.

- - - - - - - - - - - - - - - -

We suggest you use seventh chords as indicated and avoid using seventh chords in measures one and five. Of course, that would be possible too. Again, let your ear be the final judge.

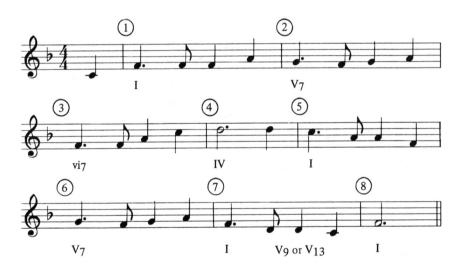

You've just harmonized a piece of music, using some complex chords. Congratulations on your progress! Now that you've come this far, you might want to try writing your own song, complete with chord progressions. Here are some guidelines to get you started (if you want to use them):

- Compose a two-part song form.
- Use the key of G-major.
- Begin with the tonic chord.
- Let the melodic curve of measures three and four resemble (or be in sequence) measures one and two.
- Use chord tones to make your melody, but throw in some nonharmonic tones so you have a good balance between conjunct and disjunct motion.
- Use this chord progression:

Part 1

①	②	③	④
I	–	IV	–

⑤	⑥	⑦	⑧
I	–	V	–

Part 2

⑨	⑩	⑪	⑫
I	–	IV	–

⑬	⑭	⑮	⑯
I	V	I	–

- Start out part two just like part one.
- Change part two (at about measure eleven) so that it begins to climb to a culmination point that was not reached in part one.
- Give the melody a mountain range quality.
- Let the overall range be at least a ninth, but not greater than an eleventh.
- Write the melody in the treble clef. Write Roman numeral chord symbols lightly in pencil below the staff.
- Write the popular music chord symbols above the staff. Use the Roman numeral chord symbols if you like.
- Play your song for friends and enjoy yourself!*

*If you'd like one of the authors of this book to critique your song, you may write to Success Dynamics for current rates. See Appendix.

Glossary

allegro -- at a running speed.

andante -- At an easy, walking speed.

Bach -- (1685--1750) a prolific 18th century German Lutheran composer. Music majors in Lutheran colleges still honor him by studying his harmonic style for two full semesters! Much of his music is tightly structured and contrapuntal in style. On the cover of this book--just for fun--we have him playing the clarinet; this may not be historically accurate! On the internet you can find his biography at http://clasicalmus.com/composers/bach.html.

beat -- a regular pulsation.

Beethoven -- (1770-1827) Beethoven studied with Mozart when he was just 17 years old. Early Beethoven sounds a lot like Mozart. Later Beethoven sounds more romantic-- it seems to have more freedom. His chord are bigger and more complex. He make more use of escape tones and unprepared dissonances. Beethoven is said to be the link between the classical and romantic styles. (We have Beethoven playing the violin on the cover of this book. It is rumored that Beethoven's father forced him to play violin for the amusement of his father's drinking buddies. The group on the cover--from left to right, Mozart, Beethoven, Bach, and Chopin--is playing music by Bartok a 20th century

Hungarian composer. But if you turn this book upside down and look at the musical score--it's also "Beach Boy's Greatest Hits, Volume 1.") For a biography of Beethoven on the internet, you may want to go to the web site at http://magic.hofstra.edu:7003/immortal/bio.html.

bridge -- In popular music, the optional contrasting section that steps away from the chorus or from the a verse. It offers new but related music and lyrical material. The beat may even shift slightly. The bridge may connect the chorus with the verse or it may separate two repetitions of the chorus at the end of a song. Often the bridge is just 8 measures long.

Chopin -- (1810-1849) a 19th century composer famously mainly for his piano music written in a lush classical romantic style. Chopin is featured on the cover of this book. He's playing the piano and checking out the rent money. See also Bach, Beethoven, and Mozart. For a biography of Chopin on the internet, you may want to refer to http://www.classicalmus.com/bmgclassics/biography/chopin.html

chord -- the simultaneous sounding of two or more tones. In traditional harmony and in popular music, a chord is usually made up of three or more different tones. But ancient composers of the Middle Ages used open sounding chords with just two notes that form the interval of a fifth. Some 20th century composers (like Aaron Copeland) have also made good use of the open fifth chords. (See chords in the index.)

chorus --the part of a song that repeats both musically and lyrically. Usually the title comes from the chorus and the song gains energy and excitement when the chorus is introduced.

chromatic -- refers to the use of tones a half-step apart. The chromatic scale is a a series of tones where each successive tone is a half-step above the previous one. In chromatic harmony, the tones of chords often progress by half-step, either up or downward.

con brio -- fast, with brilliance.

con spirito -- fast with spirit.

cresc. (crescendo) -- gradual increase in volume. Some say that musical tones should always have either a slight crescendo or diminuendo (decrease in volume) ; this gives the tones a feeling of life and movement. Often computer generated music is quite static with no crescendo or diminuendo, which makes it sound mechanical and lifeless.

deceptive cadence --a chord progression where the dominant unexpectedly moves to a chord other than the tonic. A common deceptive cadence is: V-vi (dominant chord to submediant)

dim. (diminuendo) -- see cresc.

dominant -- (1) the fifth tone of the scale. (2) a chord built on the fifth tone

of the scale. The dominant chord has a strong pull toward the tonic chord.

enharmonic -- having the same pitch, but a different spelling. For example, A-flat and G-Sharp are enharmonic equivalents.

half-step -- on the piano, the distance between a key and an adjacent key (whether black or white) .

harmony -- the "science" of putting tones together to form chords, of deciding which chord best follows another chord and how the voices in the chords can smoothly move from one chord to another.

hook -- the most memorable part of a song that hooks a listener. The hook often appears in the chorus or title section. The hook may be an exciting melodic part played by an instrument or an usual lyric. It's the part you find yourself humming after the song finishes.

interval -- the distance (measured in half-steps) between two tones. An important musical skill is the ability to listen to two notes and be able to identify and name the interval between them. This is useful in playing by ear, conducting, composing, singing, and in just getting more out of listening to music for fun. See Chapter Five, page 104. Also, on the internet, see http://www.ilovemusic.com.

key -- (or keynote) usually this refer to the tonal center of a piece of music. If a piece is written in the key of A, it means that the tonal center is the note "A." The first note of the scale will be "A."

If the piece ends with a strong sense of finality, the final chord will have "A" as it's root.

leading tone -- (1) the seventh degree of the scale. The leading tone is so named because it has a strong tendency to lead upward to the tonic. (2) A chord built on the seventh degree of the scale. This chord is often dominant in function and is often though of as dominant-seventh chord with an omitted root. (2) a chord built on the seventh tone of the scale. Important chord voicing tip: avoid doubling the leading tone whenever possible.

mediant -- (1) the third degree of the scale (2) a chord built on the third degree of the scale. The mediant is a tone of rest. It doesn't have a tendency to move very much. Still, the mediant chord is thought by some music theorists to be dominant in character since it contains two of the tones of the dominant chord. Others see it as tonic in character since it is like a tonic seventh chord with omitted root. The mediant is so named because it is mid way between the two strongest chords of the scale: the tonic and the dominant. A strong chord progression is to follow the mediant chord by submediant.

metronome -- a device for keeping time invented by a dude named Metzel. To honor Metzel, some classical composers put an abbreviation like MM=72 in their musical score. This means, "Set Metzel's metronome to 72 beats per minute. Computer software programs (sequencers) have a metronome option. If you turn on the metronome, the program will sound a regular tone (or drum beat) to help you sense the beat.

(In San Francisco, the Metronome-- (often incorrectly called the "Metrodome"--is a ballroom dance studio -- so named, I guess because the dance teachers are so good at staying on the beat. (On the cover of this book you can see an old-fashioned metronome on right side of the piano.)
moderato -- at a moderate tempo.

motive -- the smallest melodic musical idea. A good way to develop a melody is to create a distinctive motive and then vary it slightly as the melody progresses. Then shift to a different motive. Then return to the original motive. By using motives you can give your melody unity. By varying the motive or introducing new motives (not too many!) you add variety to your melody. The key is to balance unity and variety. See page 168.

Mozart -- (1756 - 1791) Mozart's music is said to be in a Classical style (as opposed to Baroque, Renaissance, or Romantic). Dissonances are introduced very carefully. Mozart's chords are simple and the texture of the music is rather thin compared to the big chords used in Romantic music. Yet Mozart was also trying to express strong emotions with his music. Today some musicians focus too much on dry precision in playing his music and miss the emotional aspects of it. I don't know if Mozart played the trumpet, but just for fun he is pictured that way on the cover of this book, on the far left. On the internet you can find information about Mozart at http://www.glasscity.net/~omoral/biography.html.

octave -- an interval that might be called an 8th. If you count up the scale from the bottom note to the top note, you would count to eight. When a pianist plays "in octaves," she plays the bottom note with her thumb and a note of the same letter name an octave higher usually with her little finger. The distance from a' to a" is an octave.

presto - very fast.

root -- the tone upon which a chord is built. See page 190.

subdominant -- (1) the fourth tone of the scale. (2) a chord built on the fourth tone of the scale. The subdominant has feeling of unrest. It wants to move either to the dominant chord or the tonic.

submediant -- (1) the sixth tone of the scale. (2) a chord built on the sixth degree of the scale. The submediant may be used as a substitute for the tonic chord. A strong progression often used at the end of a piece is V-I, or the dominant chord followed by the tonic chord. So you can give a pleasant surprise by substituting the submediant chord for the tonic like this: V - vi. This is called a deceptive cadence. Because the submediant is often substituted for the tonic (and since it has two tones in common with the tonic) it is often considered to be tonic in function.

syncopation -- putting an accent where it is not normally expected or failing to put an accent where it is expected. NOTE: Some dance teachers say, "In music, syncopation means splitting the beat into two parts." Don't believe them. See page 58.

tempo -- the speed of the beat.

tonic -- (1) the first note of the scale. (2) a chord built on the first note of the scale. The tonic chord a strong, solid feeling. This chord is used to end a piece when a strong clear ending is desired. It is also used to end a music phrase is a firm manner.

triad -- a chord made up on three notes. In traditional harmony, each successive note added to a chord is a third above the previous one.

verse -- the part of a song that has a metrical pattern and melody that repeats with different words.

verse/bridge structure -- a popular song structure without a chorus where each verse contains the song title. It is similar to "AABA "or tripartite song form in classical music. See page 184. The song begins with two verses, both of which end with the title. (That's the "AA" part. Then comes a contrasting "B" section (which appears only once) followed by a strong return to the melody of the verse with the title appearing for the third time.

verse/chorus structure -- a structure often used in popular songs. The song begins with a verse (or sometimes two). After verse comes a chorus. This structure repeats: verse, chorus; verse, chorus, etc. Each verse will have different lyrics, but the same melody. But when the chorus repeats, the same or nearly the same lyrics and melody are used.

vivace -- lively.

Index

Accents, 57-58
agogic,
rhythm, 167-168
Accidentals, 18-26, 141
Alphabet, musical, 16
Arpeggio, 209
Aural, training of, 212
Beam, 33
Beat, 44
duration of, 28
and measure, 49-50
and note value, 45, 46
patterns of, 46, 47
and pulse, 50-51
and syncopation, 60-61
value of 28
Beethoven, L. von, 41, 42
Cadence, 175
and melodic contour, 175,
176
Chords (see also Triads):
augmented, 200
construction of, 190-191
diminished, 210
doubling, 198-199
eleventh, 206, 212
from fifths, 214
interval relation to, 104
inversions, 193, 194
minor, 210
names, 192
new approaches to, 214-215
ninth, 204-205, 212
positions of, 209
progressions of, 222
guidelines for, 222-226
types of, 222-226
quartel, 214
root of, 196,209
seventh of 210-211,245
inversions of, n 2202-203
kinds of, 203-204
spacing, 194-195
guidelines for, 195-196
tertiary, 204
thirteenth, 207-212
tones of, 191
Clefs, 9
letter names, 9-10

Consonance, 155
Contour, 160-162, 173, 183
"Mountain Range," 161-
162
and song form, 182-183

Degrees, of scale, 1363-152
function and position of,
136-152
dominant, 142
leading tone, 139, 159
mediant, 147
subdominant, 149
submediant, 151
supertonic, 152
tonic (see also Keynote),
137
Dissonance, 155
relation to tone, 109
stability of 154-155
Dots, and note value
alteration, 39-40
Duration (see also Notes):
of dotted notes, 39-40
Dvorak, A., 1866-187
Echapee (see Escape tone)
Enharmonics, 22
relation between two notes,
22
Equivalents(see
Enharmonics)
Escape tone, 240-241
Fermata, 42
Fifths, circle of, 81
function in chord, 192
in harmonic intervals, 107
and intervals of, 120-121
perfect, 131
and seventh chords, 202
Flag, eighth notes and, 33
Flats, 19-20
double, 23-26
and keyboard placement,
20-21
and key signature
placement, 90-91
Form (see also Part, Phrase):
song, 180
compound, 185
three-part, 180-181
Fundamental, 145
Harmonics, 144
Harmonization, melodic,
226-230
and tertiary chords, 248
Intervals, 72,104, 162
augmented, 111-115
aural aids for identifying,
126-132
self teaching, 133

compound, 115-116
diminished, 111-115
harmonic, 106-107
inversions of, 116-118
calculating, 118-119
chords and, 209
melodic, 106
naming, 107-115
reading, 120-126
Inversions, of chords, 109
Keynote(see also Tonic):
and diatonic scales, 76
and intervals, 110
keys, of major scales, 83
of minor scales, (see
Relative major and minor)

remembering, 89
using signature of, 86,88
Letters, designations for
notes, 13
Lines, 11
ledger, 11
staff, 7
remembering, tools for, 14
separating measures, 47
Major (see under specific
headings)
Measures, 47
beats per, 49, 52
Melody,
affect of scale degrees
upon, 148
contour, 160-162
harmonization of, 226-229
simultaneous, 230
units of, 168
Meter, 44
asymmetric, 56-57
and beat patterns, 46-47
compound, 48
duple, 48
quadruple, 48
triple, 48
Metronome, 54
and tempo, 54
Minor (see under specific
headings)
Mode, and diatomic scales,
76-77
other, 97-98
Modulation, 82
Motion, 164
conjunct, 164-166
disjunct, 164-166

Motive(see also Phrase), 168-169
Music(see also Notes):
Notation, 29-37
  performance of, 162-163
  reading intervals in, 123
Naturals, 23
Notes, 7-14
  application of, 34-35
  dotted, 39, 138-139
  duration, 28
  eighth, 33
  half, 29
  quarter, 31
  sixteenth, 36
  values of, 36
  whole, 29

Notation, 7-17
Octave, 16, 108, 132, 137
  keyboard placement and, 16
  and singing, 17

Overtones, 145
  application, 147

Part, 175

Partial (see Harmonics)

Phrase, 168, 176, 180
  application of, 174
  variations, 174-175

Pitch, range of, 162-163
Primes, 13
Progression (see Chords)
Pulse, 50
Resolution, 156
  of consonance, 156-158
  of dissonance, 156-158

Rests, 40-43
  and note equivalents, 41

Rhythm, 27-29
  and duration, 28
  tree of, 37
  and unity, 167

Root, of chord, 191

Scale, 69-70, 137
  building, 70-71
  chromatic, 100- 102
  degrees of, 109-100, 154
  diatonic, 75-77
  major, 77-78
  minor, 92-97
  harmonic, 92-93

melodic, 92-93, 152
  natural, 92-93
  pentatonic, 72
  related, 80
  relative major, 95-96
  relative minor, 95-96
  relative stability of, 154-155
  and triads, 220-222
  whole tone, 99
Sequence, 183
  of phrases, 177-180

Series, harmonic, 144
Sharps, 21, 89-90
  double, 23-26
  meaning of, 21
  placement, 21
Signature, 47
  and key, 86-88
  and time, 47

Signs, harmonic, 19-23
  flats, 19
  naturals, 23
  sharps, 21

Spaces, 14

Staff, 7-15
  and F-clef, 14-15
  and G-clef, 15
  grand, 12

Stems, and note alteration 29-31

Steps, 72-73
  half, 72-73
  interval, 72-73
  whole, 72-73

Streisand, B., 64-65

Suspensions, 236-239
  and seventh chords, 247

Syncopation, 58,59, 61-62,66
  music using, 64-65
  within the beat, 61-62

Tempo, 44, 52
  application of, 55
  estimating, 54-55
  indications of, 52-53
  and performance, 44-45
  variations in, 53-54

Third, 121, 191
  intervals of, 121

Tie, and note value alteration, 38-39

Time, (see also Duration):
  common or cut, 52

Tonality, 155-156

Tones (see also Degree, Steps):
  anticipation, 241-242
  appogiatura, 239
  escape, 240-241
  neighbor, 234-236
  nonharmonic, 231
  passing, 232-234
  suspension of, 236-239

Tonic (see also Keynote), 136

Triad (see also Chords):
  analyzing, 196
  augmented, 200
  diminished, 200, 210
  major, 208
  minor, 220
  in popular music, 208
  in seventh chords, 210

Trio, 185
  and compound song from, 185

Tritone, 130-158

Tune (see Melody)

Unison, 108

Units, melodic, 168-180

Variation, 171-173
  of melody, 166
  of motive, 167-171

Vibration, 142-143
  and harmonic series, 144